BARBARA CARTLAND

BARBARA
CARTLAND
Crusader in Pink

HENRY CLOUD

EVEREST HOUSE *Publishers*
NEW YORK

To Barbara
with love and amazement

Contents

Illustrations

BARBARA CARTLAND

The 'Factory'

Since 1950 the centre of Barbara Cartland's world has been a country house called Camfield Place lying in four hundred enviable acres of park and woodland just off the A1 motorway from London to the North.

The countryside around is not immediately romantic or impressive. It is so close to London here that the suburbs are steadily encroaching: former country lanes are dotted now with filling stations, transport cafés, newly-built housing estates.

But first appearances can be deceptive. Less than five miles away is Hatfield House, one of the most splendid great Elizabethan houses in the country. Since the middle ages, Kings and Queens had hunted here, and one of Barbara's favourite gifts is a perspex paperweight containing a gilded oak-leaf picked from a tree behind her house. The following brief legend is printed on the back:

A leaf from the pages of history. This leaf has been picked from the OAK planted by Queen Elizabeth the First of England on the spot where she killed her first stag circa 1550 in the beautiful grounds of Camfield Place, Hatfield, Hertfordshire, the home of the famous authoress, Barbara Cartland. Preserved for ever in 22-carat gold.

Camfield Place itself appears a sort of enclave from the past, preserved and embellished, like the leaf, with a touch of Barbara Cartland. The railings and the cottage on the estate are painted Nile Blue (one of Barbara's favourite colours), there are handsome Park Gates (also gilded), and although the house itself – built by Beatrix Potter's grandfather – is stolidly Victorian, once past the front door you are in a world that could provide the setting for one of her own romantic novels.

The imposing downstairs rooms are banked with flowers, and the pictures are distinguished: a fine eighteenth-century hunting scene by Webb and various other portraits of her late husband's Granville ancestors. For many years Barbara collected gilt rococo tables and four-poster beds, and the effect is happily flamboyant, making the interior appear an impromptu treasure-house, larger than life, distinctly glamorous, the natural background it would seem for the world's most successful romantic lady novelist.

But Camfield Place is really two houses in one, and nobody can be here long without becoming rapidly aware of it. From the entrance hall the second door on the left leads off to the secretarys' office, and here every inch of space is crammed with typing desks and filing cabinets and stacks of the latest Barbara Cartlands hot from the publishers. The walls are lined from floor to ceiling with framed originals of Francis Marshall's paintings for the jackets of the books, and four permanent secretaries work here five days a week. There is the sharp electric spark of business in the air. This is the part of Camfield Place that someone dubbed the 'Factory'.

Barbara's life inevitably divides between these two aspects of the house. Weekends are for her family and friends, and in particular for her two sons Ian and Glen who are the two most important people in her life. Ian, aged forty, a bonhomous, deceptively easy-going man, is married, with two young daughters and acts as his mother's business manager, directing her affairs with breezy acumen through a partnership called Cartland Promotions. He is an efficient businessman and has made a lot of money for, 'my wonderful mother'. Barbara herself is very vague about her earnings and always says, 'Oh you must ask Ian that', in answer to any questions on finance.

Glen is aged thirty-eight, unmarried and a London stockbroker. He is a shyer, more romantic character than his brother, and advises his mother on her books, which he is the first to read in manuscript. Barbara's eldest child, her daughter Raine, now Countess Spencer, inevitably leads a separate life as mistress of Althorp, one of the stateliest of England's stately homes, and wife of one of the richest landowners in the country. But Ian and Glen, although they live in London, are usually at Camfield Place for the weekend. They shoot there during the pheasant season, help their mother entertain her guests and give her what she most enjoys in life – the feeling that her family are actively involved in everything she does.

Barbara lives in style, as few of her Dukes would manage to these days. She is not personally extravagant but the house is expensive to maintain, and it pleases her to run it like a comfortable Edwardian country house. She has her white Rolls-Royce, which she calls 'my trade-mark', her butler, and her chef.

It was typical of her to send her chef, Nigel Gordon, off to eat in several of the finest restaurants 'to see how food should look', and the weekend food at Camfield Place is very good indeed. Barbara herself has no pretensions as a cook – although she has written several cook books – but she believes strongly in the importance of nourishment, particularly protein, for healthy living and real happiness.

Men, she has written, require 'regular feeding and a diet abundant in protein to keep them in condition'. So do women, and she makes sure that at Camfield Place they get it. Nigel Gordon's specialities include Salmon Coulibiac, game from the estate and perfect soufflés. Barbara herself eats modestly, but strongly disagrees with women who starve themselves in an attempt to keep thin. 'It could do untold damage to their health,' she says, 'and anyhow, I've yet to meet a man who didn't like a handful.'

From Monday to Friday Barbara conducts her life according to a tightly disciplined routine, and it is now that the 'Factory' takes over. In this she is aided by her secretary, Mrs Waller, an attractive, quietly efficient woman in her early thirties who comes closer than anyone to running Barbara's life. Not that this is always possible, for Barbara is incapable of delegating and so hyper-energetic that there is little that she does not try to do herself. 'If only people would accept that I'm *always* right,' she says, 'everything would go like clockwork.'

But Ruth Waller is one of the marvels of Camfield Place. For despite the fact that Barbara maintains that it is very different to work with women, her secretaries are the exception. 'They are a marvellous team – my lifeline,' she says. Mrs Waller has been acting as a sort of general manager for the 'Factory' for the last thirteen years. Barbara, half-jokingly, refers to her as 'my Comptroller'. 'Royalty have Comptrollers who see to the details of their lives. That's what Ruth Waller does with mine.'

Barbara is called at eight forty-five sharp, by a ladysmaid who has been with her for thirty-five years. Sleep is another thing that Barbara believes in. 'Most people need eight hours a night, especially if they use their brain. My family all need a lot of sleep and I have always believed it important for them at weekends to sleep until they wake.' She is generally in bed by nine o'clock at night and reads for an hour or so before she goes to sleep. Similarly she deals with her post, the morning papers and her breakfast in bed. With her breakfast comes a most important part of her routine – the seventy or so vitamin pills and capsules to which she ascribes her extraordinary vitality and health.

Not for Barbara the pleasure of a casual, easy-going morning. There are thirty or forty letters to which she dictates a reply and endless telephone calls before she has her bath. Each day is treated like a grand occasion, in which Barbara always has the starring part. She always dresses glamorously – Cartland pink or brilliant blue – and insists that she does this purely to please herself.

By now it is eleven-thirty and Barbara descends and takes her two dogs for a walk. One is a white lion Pekingese called Twi-Twi – who featured in her recent novel, *The Prince and the Pekingese* – the other a black Labrador, appropriately christened Duke, who was born at Broadlands and given to Barbara by her great friend, Earl Mountbatten of Burma. The dogs have come to form a sort of symbol of the two opposed elements in Barbara's life. Twi-Twi is cosseted, luxurious and bites strangers; Duke is down-to-earth, extrovert and wags his tail at everyone he meets.

Lunch on a working day is simpler than at weekends, and Barbara eats the same menu as is provided for her secretaries, sitting alone at the head of her immaculately laid and polished dining-table. Then, just after one o'clock, the most important part of her day begins.

She walks from the dining-room, followed by her dogs, across the hall and into Grandpa Potter's big library which holds over three thousand of the books she has collected for research. There she makes herself comfortable on a big yellow-brocade sofa in front of the fire – a hot-water-bottle at her feet and over her legs a pink rug covered in white fur.

Mrs Audrey Elliott, her literary secretary, sits behind her, pad in hand. As an extra safeguard a tape-recorder is switched on. And for the next two-and-a-half hours, Barbara dictates a chapter of her latest novel. Apart from her very earliest novels, and her 'serious' books, like the lives of her mother, her brother, Ronald, and eight historical biographies, she has dictated all her books. It was Godfrey Winn who first advised her to do this : 'The words you speak are so much more immediate and sincere than those you write,' he explained to her – invaluable advice.

For she has taught herself the virtuoso art of unhesitating dictation. It requires extraordinary powers of concentration, and Mrs Elliott, apart from being very accurate, has long discovered how to remain invisible and totally discreet throughout the process. Sitting directly behind Barbara, all Barbara can see of her is the faint reflection of her face in the glass of the bookcases beyond. It is an uncanny scene as Barbara – makeup still immaculate, hair perfectly in place, a string of pearls around her neck – starts to construct her latest book.

She herself describes the process : 'As I sit there I'm simply telling myself a story, and I am told my voice changes as I take each separate part – I see exactly what is happening as I describe it and I live through each dramatic incident. I've always had this unusually vivid visual imagination, and I can really see each room my characters are in.

'The dining-rooms I use are versions of the dining-room from my grandfather's Georgian house which I remember as a child, the famous ancestral houses in which I stayed or have visited and places where I've actually been. This is why my books are very lifelike.'

'And what about your heroine?' one asks.

'Oh, she is always me, and always virginal of course. She's something of a Cinderella, and I've always thought the point where a young girl falls in love just on the edge of womanhood is the most romantic moment in her life.

'Whenever I've had a love affair myself I've always somehow felt I was innocent. It is a sort of mental virginity – that lovely feeling that real love has happened to me for the very first time. I think most women secretly enjoy this idealistic sensation and I try to get it into all my books.'

'And your heroes?'

'Of course they're the sort of men I've always found attractive – tall, dark and rather challenging. They're expert lovers, quite unlike my heroines of course, and I always particularly enjoy the part where the heroine makes it clear that she doesn't quite know what goes on in bed, and the hero says: "Darling, that is something I will explain later," which he does on the page when they're safely married.'

One of the most phenomenal things about her work is that she never seems to falter, never needs to correct herself – and never fails. She cheerfully admits she cannot spell and that her punctuation could improve, but incidentals such as these are taken care of by a retired classics master who reads each manuscript before it is finally retyped for the publisher.

Another extraordinary thing about her work is the speed with which she can construct a book. Her theme, as she explains, is traditional. The Cinderella virgin meets and falls in love with her challenging dark hero on the first few pages. Events occur to mar or complicate the course of true love for the next six chapters. But in the seventh, love wins through, the pair are safely married, and we leave them as the joys of licit carnal bliss are just about to start.

But after a lifetime writing just this sort of book, Barbara's skill consists in the endless ingenuity with which she adapts this constant theme to different historic backgrounds and events. Her period extends from the 1790s, when men stopped wearing wigs – 'I never really believe a man in a wig could be an attractive lover,' she explains – until the death-knell of Edwardian England. For locales she has scoured the world, from Haiti and South America, to Bali and St Petersburg.

But every book is carefully authentic in its background and she reckons that she reads twenty to thirty serious history books for each novel. These are collected by her chauffeur from the London Library or Hatchard's, or provided by the local County Librarians who take a personal interest in her requirements.

As one might expect, she reads extremely fast. 'You have to understand,' she says, 'that I have had to educate myself, so I enjoy learning about a period and then weaving myself a lovely romantic story round it all.'

. And weave she does, six to seven thousand words an afternoon, forty-five thousand words a book – and after seven afternoons with Mrs Elliott behind her, the book is finished and only has to be typed by Mrs Clark whose manuscripts, Barbara says, are the best any publisher or editor has ever seen. 'I expect, and get perfection,' she adds.

Barbara shows no sign of author's strain throughout this period, no nerves, no hesitation. According to Mrs Waller she is more relaxed and energetic after an afternoon's dictation than she was before. It is only when she is not involved in a book that she begins to get restless.

For Barbara lives her books and they have now become a crucial part of her existence. She believes implicitly in what she writes, and this is the key to their success, the vital quality she shares with every really big, mass-selling author of popular fiction – sincerity. It is impossible to counterfeit and pointless to deride. Edgar Wallace had it, so did Ian Fleming, so does Barbara – the ability to turn their private dreams into the sort of myth that has a universal appeal. In Barbara's case, this appeal is still increasing, as her books are read by countless million female – and male – readers of all ages, classes, and levels of intelligence, from Tokyo to Trinidad, San Francisco to Ceylon, Britain to Brazil.

But what really are these dreams which have such universal feminine appeal? And where did they begin?

CHAPTER TWO

Polly's World

Barbara is not a snob – 'Give me an interesting dustman rather than a boring Duke to talk to any day,' she says – but as a romantic novelist she is predictably keen on noble antecedents.

The downstairs cloakroom at Camfield Place has a large framed family tree tracing her husband's family back, via the Granvilles, to Duke Rollo, grandfather of William the Conqueror, and she has written proudly of the way her mother's family, the Scobells, are descended from 'one of the oldest Saxon families in Great Britain', the de Scoberhulls who were High Sheriffs of Devon in the years before the Norman Conquest.

She finds such connections, like the Dukes and Marquises she writes about, 'very romantic'; but her own immediate past lies not with the upper aristocracy. Like many writers of her period, she comes from that most fertile of imaginative seed-beds, the dispossessed Edwardian gentry.

One of her prized possessions is an imposing marble bust of her maternal grandfather, Colonel George Scobell, which glares at visitors across the hall of Camfield Place. Even in marble he could almost be a Barbara Cartland hero with his handsome commanding profile, perceptive, searching eyes and bold, sardonic whiskers.

True, he was not a Duke, but a Rector's son from Sussex, who was sent to Winchester and Trinity College, Oxford, and inherited a small fortune from an unmarried naval uncle who was a Member of Parliament and invented the V C. This enabled George Scobell to travel widely, climb Mont Blanc, and make love to a lot of women of all sizes, shapes and nationalities, before marrying in the early 1870s.

His bride, Edith Palairet, enjoyed an income of £2,000 a year and was connected with the Hamiltons of Philadelphia – and thence with the Dukes of Hamilton. She was a lively, energetic, tolerant lady – which was just as well, for Colonel Scobell's interest in the fair sex did not cease with marriage.

The Scobells lived in considerable style in Down House, Redmarley, a village some ten miles from Worcester. It was a graceful, many bedroomed Georgian mansion, with its own farm and small estate, and the Colonel – he served loyally for many years with the local militia – employed twelve indoor servants, four men in the gardens, three in the stables, and six on the farm. Most years he reckoned to make a profit of at least two hundred pounds from his land.

He hunted five days a week, fathered four daughters and one son, and remained something of a fire-eater to the day he died, imposing order and obedience upon his family by the sheer strength of his extremely dominating personality. It was a religious household, and a very ordered one – with the Colonel taking family prayers at eight o'clock each morning.

But the Colonel was a restless, frequently irascible character, always dreaming of fresh Mont Blancs to climb. And it was into this little High Victorian kingdom which he ruled so absolutely, that Barbara's mother was born in 1877. She was the fourth daughter – and the Colonel's reactions to her sex can be imagined. She was duly christened Mary Hamilton, but throughout her long and very energetic life, was always known as Polly.

Even in extreme old age – she failed to reach her century by a mere three years, and died in 1974 – Polly Cartland was remembered for her extraordinary vitality and zest for life. She was a bright-eyed, saintly little lady, and one visitor to Camfield Place remembers her, aged ninety-five, 'still whizzing around the place like a torpedo'.

A Catholic convert during the last years of her life, her goodness and concern for others were a local legend in the village outside Malvern where she lived. But what really made her what she was, throughout her long and often daunting life, was sheer indomitable courage. Nothing defeated her – neither poverty, nor disappointment, nor the sudden death of those she loved. Through each disaster of her life, she managed to uphold the standards she had learned to value and to live by in her childhood. And like many very virtuous people she imposed these standards powerfully on those she loved.

Disaster dogged her all her life, and the first occurred soon after her marriage, early in 1900, to the handsome, very dashing Bertram Cartland. Until this point, Polly's life had been extremely happy, sheltered and conventional, and Bertie Cartland was exactly the sort of personable rich young man that girls like Polly always fell in love with.

But Colonel Scobell disapproved, on the grounds that the Cartlands were not country gentry with that all-important stake in the land, but financiers – and Birmingham financiers at that, having made their considerable fortune out of brass-founding and then from business speculation.

This was very bad, of course. But Polly was thoroughly in love by now and had a good streak of her father's obstinacy too. Against great opposition she married her good-looking Bertie, but instead of discovering the happiness she dreamed of, her father's fears were rapidly proved right.

The young couple had barely settled into a charming house in the Worcestershire countryside, when all hopes of that comfortable, wealthy life they had been counting on were blighted. Bertie's father, James Cartland, had invested heavily in his plan to build the Fishguard Railway. There was a brief financial panic, the bank pulled in its loans, and the luckless financier discovered overnight that he was ruined.

Rather than face a straitened future on a mere £6,000 a year –

over £100,000 in today's inflated currency – James Cartland took the time-honoured course prescribed for ruined Victorian businessmen. He promptly shot himself – and by taking what was considered the honourable way out, inflicted years of hardship on the newly-weds.

For by July 1901 they already had a child – Barbara – and were totally dependent on the allowance they had been receiving from Bertie's father for their agreeable existence to continue. Bertie could play polo, gamble, drink and ride like any gently raised Edwardian gentleman of means – but suddenly there were no means. What followed then had all the makings of a classic period catastrophe.

Since their house unfortunately belonged to James Cartland's estate, Bertie had no power to prevent it being sold above their heads. His horses followed. There were naturally appeals to Colonel Scobell, but he declined to help when he learned of Bertie's gambling debts, and chronic inability to work. Tears, dramas, misery ensued and when all the dust had settled, one small person kept the little family afloat – the indomitable undefeatable Polly.

She was the one who found a suitable house that they could just afford. It sounded rather grander than it was, for Amerie Court was no more than a simple farmhouse on the Earl of Coventry's estate at Pershore. With a total income of under £300 a year there was no money now for more than one servant and a nanny for Barbara. Polly's task was simply to ensure that they survived – which she did by such expedients as packaging the sweet Pershore plums which she and Bertie picked from the orchard, and selling them by post to friends in London.

But Polly had a more important aim than the mere survival of her family. Her greatest concern of all was to ensure that she and Bertie did not lose their friends. Their situation was unfortunate, but she had no intention of sinking into shabby obscurity.

'My friends have always been wonderful to me,' she said all her life, but she received what she gave.

'My mother's pride and high standards kept her going,' says Barbara, 'and the invincible courage she showed all through her difficult and often tragic life.'

These 'standards' which Polly had known as a girl were all-important, and had to be carefully maintained. Pride demanded it. The few remaining bits of silver with the Cartland crest were ritually polished and displayed upon the sideboard. Old friends like the Cavendish-Bentincks, the Beauchamps and the Coventrys were invited to dinner before the Hunt Balls, and luncheon before the Pershore races — although this always meant that Polly had to work for days to have everything as she had known it as a girl.

She even managed to continue hunting once or twice a week, even if it did mean cycling a good eight miles to the hunt. The Master of Foxhounds provided her with a mount.

So Polly never did lose her friends. Her pluck and charm effectively made certain that she kept her friends. And like the Victorian Lady Bountiful she had been brought up to be, she continued to do good works among the local poor almost until the day she died.

After Barbara there were two more children — Ronald, who was born in January 1907 and a second son, Tony, born in 1913. Polly's influence upon her children was not unlike old Colonel Scobell's, for she was a stickler for etiquette. As she herself recalled in a radio interview towards the end of her life,

I was very particular myself about manners. I taught the children from a very early age how to behave at table and how the boys should always open doors for people, and particularly for their sister. I didn't allow any sloppiness. We all changed for dinner — no sitting down anyhow or anything like that. You see, I had been brought up in a grand house, very strictly, and I wouldn't have anyone just rushing in to dinner in their ordinary clothes.

But Polly's most extraordinary achievement was her recla-
mation of her husband. By sheer force of will – and the power of
all-enfolding love – she seems to have saved him from despair and
pulled him firmly to his senses. Under her impressive influence he
became ambitious. Somehow she coped with his debts – after a
tearfully extracted promise of no more gambling.

More important still, it was really thanks to her, and her ceaseless
efforts to keep going that Bertie got the chance he needed. She and
Bertie were invited to attend a Conservative dinner specially to
meet their prospective Parliamentary candidate, Cdr Bolton
Eyres-Monsell from Dumbleton Hall, Evesham, who was married
to an extremely wealthy heiress from Leeds. There was a lot of
talk about the need for a local political organiser. Polly suggested
Bertie for the position – and largely thanks to the support of the
Coventrys, he became Honorary Secretary of the local Primrose
League. It was the start of his career in politics.

For what nobody but Polly realised was that Bertie actually
possessed unsuspected talents as a politician. He could speak well –
particularly when previously rehearsed by Polly. More important
still, he was an effective organiser and by the beginning of the
1909 General Election, he was running the whole campaign.
Eyres-Monsell got in by 1,400 votes – and from this point it
seemed as if the fortunes of the Cartland family were picking up
at last.

In gratitude for Bertie's work in the election, Eyres-Monsell and
his wife invited the Cartlands for a holiday in Switzerland as their
personal guests. They stayed for a night or two in the Monsells'
house in Belgrave Square, then had a fortnight at the fashionable
resort of Engelberg in the Swiss Alps. They skated, skied, and got
to know a number of the Monsells' friends – including a shy
politician from another part of Worcestershire called Stanley
Baldwin, and his cousin, Rudyard Kipling.

Kipling and Bertie got on rather well together – so did Polly
and Stanley Baldwin. The holiday was deemed a great success, and

in Eyres-Monsell Polly now had what she needed — a personal friend who could help Bertie politically. The friendship deepened and, a few months later, Monsell invited Bertie to become his Political Secretary at a salary of £150 a year. Bertie was starting to succeed, and within a year had taken on the organisation of five counties for the Primrose League, making him a very busy man indeed.

His next step up the ladder of success came early in 1914 when it was decided to evacuate 10,000 Protestant women and children to avoid a bloodbath when rebellion threatened Ulster. Preliminary arrangements were chaotic, and Bertie was recommended to sort out the muddle — which he did with great efficiency.

But even more important were the social opportunities which Bertie's new success was offering the Cartlands. There were the shooting parties and the balls at Dumbleton, the Primrose League teas at Amerie Court, contacts with many well-known politicians and their wives. Polly was in her element. She had survived those grim disasters of the early years of marriage. The years of effort had been proved worth while, those 'standards' she so ardently believed in had been vindicated.

There were even plans for Bertie to go in to Parliament himself one day. Then came the war to put an end to all such golden dreams.

This was the world of Barbara's childhood and one can see her in the photographs in the family albums for this period which Polly religiously kept — a solemn, long-haired, self-possessed small girl, sitting alone in the garden at Amerie Court, or holding her well-scrubbed brother, Ronald, firmly by the hand.

Included with the photographs, Polly has preserved the first story Barbara wrote — aged five. It is copied out in crayon, and has the title boldly written on the front page:

The Little Slide Maker
by
Barbara Cartland.

Once upon a time there was a little girl and her name was Mary.

Now this little girl was very fond of making slides.

Her father was the village doctor.

One evening the Doctor came home late.

Mr Joe Carter stepped into a slide. Poor old man. He said I hope no slide will be made down Winter Hill or it will be a bad look out for old Betsy Gray.

Then Mary felt very unhappy for it was just down Winters Hill that she had made all her slides. That evening when she had been put to bed she got up and got a spade. When she got to the hill she found that the dirt at the side of the road was quite hard but she found some in a garden at the top of the hill.

The End.

Barabara was clearly an intelligent girl and one can understand the all-important influences that she was now absorbing from her family — and particularly from Polly. There was that exciting splendour of life in a grand Georgian house which she remembered as a small girl in her visits to her grandfather, the forbidding Colonel Scobell — and there were even grander houses for her still to visit, owned by her mother's friends. 'I have always found something profoundly moving and romantic in ancient houses', she explains. 'They form an important background for my books.'

But, more important still were the actual lessons she was learning from her mother — the importance of the family, and the role of manners and conventional Edwardian morality. And most intriguing of all, for the development of Barbara's philosophy of life, was Polly's example of the power of the woman in the home. She managed to enshrine the Edwardian myth of the tender, loving, feminine woman – and used these qualities to rule the wayward male in her life.

Then with the war Polly had a different task. Bertie was thirty-eight and could easily have found himself a job at the War Office or behind the lines. But Polly was too patriotic to encourage any husband to such ignominious behaviour. Bertie would do his duty – so would Polly. It was a woman's task to bear parting bravely, and to inspire her husband to become a hero. And this she did with Bertie.

Late that October Polly travelled to Southampton to see her husband off to France. He had been commissioned in the Worcester Regiment and before he left they had a few magical days together.

One charming friend of the Monsells they had met at Dumbleton was Wilfred Ashley, the widowed son-in-law of the great Edwardian financier, Sir Ernest Cassel. He lived at Broadlands, the magnificent eighteenth-century house at Romsey which had once belonged to Palmerston, and invited the Cartlands to spend Bertie's embarkation leave with him.

It was an unforgettable event for Polly, and would have fascinating echoes too for Barbara later in her life. Polly and Bertie were charmed by the handsome Mr Ashley, thrilled by the splendours of the house, and particularly taken by their host's two motherless daughters, Edwina and Mary. On the Sunday, Polly took the little girls to church. Later she told Barbara that, 'she thought Edwina very pretty and intelligent, but Mary, thin and rather peaked, with red hair, looked wistful and as if she needed mothering'. A few days later, Bertie was in France.

Despite his age, Bertie had a distinguished war as an infantry officer in France, and was mentioned in despatches 'for gallant and distinguished service in the field'. Early in 1917, after some months of illness, he was offered the post of Garrison Adjutant at Folkestone. It was a post that would have suited him – and by almost any reckoning he had earned himself a break after his time in France. But even now there was Polly's estimation to consider. He still had to make her proud of him and do what he felt to be his duty. And so largely for Polly's sake he turned down Folkestone and early in the summer of 1917 was back in the trenches yet again.

He was promoted Major and survived the dangers and discomforts of the front line for a year. At times he wrote that he was 'miserably depressed . . . and awfully homesick (wife-sick)!' But Polly's love was still his inspiration, and one of his constant hopes was still to win a medal that would make her proud of him, although as he wrote somewhat sadly, 'One is too old really to be ambitious for mere gauds and baubles, especially when you see how these are dished out.'

He never got his medal, but was killed with the rest of his battalion in the last big German push of May 1918.

It was a hero's death. For Polly the agony was doubled when, a whole month after the report of her husband's death in action, she received a telegram from the War Office saying he was not killed, merely 'missing'. The uncertainty dragged on almost until the Armistice when his death was finally confirmed.

But Polly never wavered. Nor did the children. For the little family it was an even worse disaster than James Cartland's death had been. Polly's high hopes were at an end. Now she would never be the wife of a Member of Parliament and never know the success she had wanted for Bertie. Life would be infinitely harder for the children too. For once again the Cartlands were extremely poor. The children lacked a father and Polly would have the task of raising them on her own.

Barbara was nearly seventeen, and away at boarding school, when she heard the first news of her father's death. Judging from the letter that she wrote to Polly, she took it rather well.

You are such a brave Mother that you will make up for all. You and Daddy were an absolutely ideal Mother and Father and you, my Angel, were a perfect *wife* and a perfect *Mother*.

I feel so awfully proud of him and in a way it's lovely to remember him so young and cheery.

But the most remarkable of all the letters of condolence Polly received came from her eleven-year-old son, Ronald, from his preparatory school near Haywards Heath.

My Angel,

Thank you so much for your two letters, Darling. I know I am the eldest son, I must be everything to you, and Pray God I shall never offend him who is dead or you, my darling. I shall soon be with you, Angel, and then I hope I shall be able to cheer you up. . . .

Of course, darling, I will follow Daddy; but will you please explain to me in your next letter what you mean by this – 'I want you to start where your Father left off'.

I wish I was at home to help you answer your two hundred letters. Darling, where shall we live now? I, being the son who should and will look after you, must know, for you, darling, are alone. There is no Daddy to keep us alive. But God will keep us.

Forgive such a short letter but I have four others to write, Darling. I will be your right hand, my dearest one.

All my love, Angel,

I am ever,

Your ever loving son,

Ronald.

Bertie's death united his small family more certainly than if he had survived. And once again, as in her early days of marriage when she inspired Bertie to achieve, Polly's great role was now to fill her children with ambition. For now, in addition to those 'standards' and beliefs which she had taught them, they had a hero father as a great example.

For her children Polly made their life appear a personal crusade.

She prayed for them, she spurred them and inspired them with her
love, and as Barbara herself has written, 'She lit a flame in all three
that was to burn brighter year by year. She made them believe in
themselves and their capabilities. She made them see that anything
was possible if they really wanted it and worked hard enough. To
Polly there were no heights that her children could not attain.'

For Ronald, even at eleven, this meant politics. Barbara remembers him a few years earlier, already copying his father by
making political speeches in the playroom – and when he had
finished, applauding himself with great enthusiasm. Tony, who
was seven, would also follow in his father's footsteps – as a soldier.

Barbara's scope for changing the world was far more limited
than her brothers' – and anyhow neither Barbara nor her mother
believed in women trying to achieve success by copying their
menfolk. Now that Barbara was nearly through her finishing
school – at Netley Abbey, Hampshire – and was already something of a beauty, there was only one right 'career' for her –
marriage. Polly prayed that she would fall deeply in love as she had,
but she also longed for Barbara to marry a man with money. She
knew only too well the problems and difficulties of poverty and
debts. She would not have been human if she had not hoped that
Barbara would have what she had lost – 'Park Gates'.

Polly was so unhappy without Bertie that it was Barbara who
decided, now she was grown up, that they should live in London.
At eighteen she was longing for excitement, fun – and lots of
young men to dance with her.

So Polly found a terraced house in Nevelle Street, South
Kensington to rent. It was almost Belgravia – if not quite Mayfair
– and several years later, to make ends meet, the resourceful Polly
opened up a shop. Before the war, of course, this would have been
unthinkable. But by the early Twenties a few smart ladies had
already realised it might be 'fun' to have a dress shop or a milliner's
and sell to their friends.

Polly followed suit. In the country she had a friend, a Vicar's spinster daughter, who was an inspired knitter and specialised in fashionable knitted dresses. Polly decided she could sell them – and opened up a little shop called 'Knitwear' in a flat in Pont Street.

Long before this, the first night the family arrived in London, Barbara and Ronald walked together up towards South Kensington underground station, and stood there, hand in hand, gazing at the lights. Suddenly their future seemed to lie before them.

'I,' said Ronald, echoing Polly's extravagant ambitions, 'I shall be Prime Minister.'

'And I,' said Barbara, 'will get to know everyone in London.'

CHAPTER THREE

The Wisest Virgin

Personally I want to be loved, adored, worshipped, cosseted and protected. Judging from the Romantic Boom, this is what women all over the world want too, and I am quite sure it is what they eventually will get. The pendulum will swing as it always does, and in five to ten years' time it will be fashionable to be a virgin.

Thus Barbara wrote, early in 1977, in a famous article for *The Times* entitled 'A Virginity Boom?' and there have been moments since when she candidly admits to growing slightly weary of the subject of virginity, especially when questioned for the umpteenth time by eager journalists trying to catch her out by asking where, if girls stay pure until their marriage night, Barbara's ideal husbands are to gain their sexual expertise.

But the point remains that female purity — and virginity in girls until they marry — forms an important part in Barbara's personal philosophy of the romantic, inspirational role of womanhood today. It is a major theme in all her books and, not surprisingly, she was a determinedly romantic and successful virgin on her own account until she married.

When she arrived in London she was the image of one of her own youthful heroines. She has described herself looking rather like a younger version of Gladys Cooper or Lily Elsie: 'There was an air of gentle unsophistication about them both which made a man feel he wanted to cherish and protect them. There was nothing frightening, hard or challenging about their looks. They were essentially feminine, womanly and sweetly pink and white.'

With her spectacularly green eyes, fluffy hair, and flawless complexion, Barbara was much the same. She was, she says, 'incredibly ignorant, not only of the world, of life, of sex, but also of politics and almost every known subject'. Not that this really mattered; rather the reverse. The innocent, demure young lady was just the sort of girl the returning servicemen had dreamed about in France. Without knowing it at first, Barbara was very much in vogue, and innocence and purity and gentle femininity formed an important part of her appeal.

There was also the fact that the Edwardian world that she was born in had made something of a fetish of the sanctity of unmarried well-brought-up young ladies. Even in the fastest set it was considered quite unthinkable for any male, however rakish, to cast his eyes upon such innocence – after the girl had married it was quite another matter – and despite the war, these attitudes persisted in polite society.

But Barbara had imbibed something more than the ordinary Edwardian moral code which Polly took for granted. She was not a prude, but something very different. At school at Netley Abbey she had learned little, but in the holidays she had read voraciously – dozens and dozens of light romantic novels: Elinor Glyn, E. M. Hull, whose book *The Sheik* had set Edwardian womanhood aquiver with dreams of an illicit passion for a desert lover, and the Queen of all romantic lady novelists, Ethel M. Dell.

The effect of all this heady literature on Barbara was dramatic, and has remained with her for life. It made her a passionate romantic, with a private dream world of her own. It also gave her a clear picture of her own feminine role, the sort of woman she would be, and the men that she would fall in love with.

Even today she is insistent on the debt she owes to Ethel M. Dell, a prolific and almost totally forgotten author.

I have copied her formula all my life. What she said was a revelation – that men were strong, silent, passionate heroes. And really my whole life has been geared to that. She believed, and I believed, that a woman, in

order to be a good woman, was pure and innocent, and that God always
answered her prayers, sooner or later.

There was a further lesson Barbara learned from Miss Dell during
the hours she spent reading the novels she borrowed at 2d. each
from a lending library. It was the most exciting and important
thought of all, the belief, as she has stated it, that 'human passions
are transformed by love into the spiritual and become part of the
divine.'

Inevitably this became at once the sort of love that she was
seeking, when she started to respond to the young men who were
so eager to take her out. Logically she should have done what
Polly really wanted her to do — make a brilliant social as well as a
happy marriage. If she could not find a Duke to fall in love with,
she should at least make sure she married Park Gates.

But for a true believer in the gospel according to Miss Dell, this
was patently impossible. Love was too pure and mystical to be
ruled by such down-to-earth considerations. And Barbara, with
her high ideals and passionate belief in love, was really seeking one
thing — that heady transformation from earthly love into the
divine which she believed was possible.

Thanks to the upheaval of the war, her search was easier than it
would have been in the world her mother knew. Many of the old
restrictions on the freedom of polite young ladies had been quietly
forgotten, and although, as Barbara says, 'the things that nice girls
couldn't do seemed endless', and it remained 'a mother's job to
protect her daughter against the virile passions of every man who
saw her', there was a great deal that *could* now go on that mothers
never knew about.

Chaperons had all but vanished, and although it was still
considered 'fast' for a nice girl to dine alone with even the nicest
of young men, there was nothing to forbid her dancing with him
afterwards. There were 'respectable' *thé dansants* at the Savoy

(although the lower-class Astoria Dance Hall was naturally taboo). There was dancing at the Grafton Galleries, with the chance of brushing shoulders with the Prince of Wales; and by 1920 there was a night club known as Rector's off the Tottenham Court Road, where one could dance till two am and the men could even buy a drink in the cloakroom. 'I was not supposed to go to Rector's,' Barbara says, 'but who could resist the temptation?'

She thoroughly enjoyed herself and lived the role that would form the inspiration of her novels – that of the Cinderella figure of the pretty, all but penniless young virgin, dancing till dawn, dreaming about her unknown Prince, and wondering if he existed among the romantically-inclined young men who fell in love with her.

Some of them had motor cars. Some could scarcely pay the taxi fare from the Guards Club to her mother's home now in Eaton Terrace. Some even swore to shoot themselves if she wouldn't marry them. But Barbara's high ideals were proof even against this sort of blackmail, and she always kept her swains in order. 'I invented a rule that I would not allow any young man to kiss me unless he had formally made me a proposal of marriage. It was a reward for virtue.'

For Barbara virtue was its own reward. As regularly as the proposals came, she turned them all down. She lived her life by the principles Miss Dell had taught her – and waited for her Prince, or his equivalent, to come along. For a brief few months the year after she left school she thought she had found him and became engaged to an Irishman, Terence, always known as Pingo, the only son of Sir Hercules Languishe, the Fifth Baronet. There was a crumbling centuries-old Castle in Ireland, but no money.

The Times published the announcement, wedding presents began to arrive, but Polly said firmly that no one could live on air. With a million men in Britain from the Services looking for work

Pingo joined the Special Police Force in Ireland. His best friend, with ten other officers, was killed on 'Bloody Sunday', and Barbara with a sudden horror of violence broke off the engagement.

Polly coped with a broken-hearted Pingo who came rushing back from Ireland to force Barbara to change her mind. Neither threats nor tears prevailed, but Polly insisted that in future there would be no official engagement until Barbara was sure of her own mind – or rather of her heart.

A year later, Polly was becoming concerned about financial difficulties. If there was no immediate Park Gates in sight, Barbara had better find herself a job. Ronald was now at Charterhouse – thanks to a financial concession for the sons of old boys killed in the war – and Polly had moved from Pont Street into larger premises, a house in Sloane Street. However, the shop, even with Polly running it, barely sufficed to pay the family bills, let alone support a grown daughter.

Polly suggested Barbara should study shorthand-typing, like many indigent but thoroughly nice young ladies of the period. Then she could find herself a suitable, respectable position as a doctor's secretary – or something of the sort. Barbara had ideas of her own upon the subject.

At several of the parties she had been to, she had got to know Richard Viner, a smooth, agreeable young man who was the Editor of the gossip column of the *Daily Express*. One evening he suggested she should contribute to it by telephoning first thing in the morning to tell him anything of interest that had happened the day before. To her surprise, she earned five shillings for each paragraph, 'which seemed an awful lot of money at the time'. It was the start of her career as a professional writer.

With most penurious young ladies, their journalistic début would have ended there and then. But Barbara was Polly Cartland's daughter, and before long she had progressed beyond the social snippet to the glories of the full-scale article, for the *Daily*

Express. All that she really had to do at first was write about herself
– and so become a sort of spokesman for the 'Bright Young People'
of the times who held such fascination for the readers of the
Express.

Her first article was boldly entitled, 'Youth Speaks Up', and the
editor, in a brief introductory note assured his readers that, 'Miss
Cartland, who is twenty-two, exemplifies in London Society the
charming and intellectually exuberant type she describes.'

Barbara took as her theme the subject of 'The Modern Girl'. It
was often used, she said, as a term of reproach,

but all that is the matter with her can be explained in one word –
enthusiasm. Youth acting on an impulse, fired with the spirit of an idea,
disregarding the consequences, demanding the compliance of its desires
in an instant, and forging ahead to attain them – who shall condemn it?

Certainly not the *Express*, and a few days later Barbara had a
chance to spread herself on a subject which has exercised her ever
since – the weaknesses of men, and the duty of women to bring
them to their senses.

The young man of today is getting slack. Just casual about making a
fool of himself. And we cannot blame him. When he drinks too much
there is no fear of his being a hopeless inebriate, but he will lose his self-
respect. It is hard to draw a hard and fast line between decency and
degradation. The remedy lies in the capable hands of the young woman
of today. Will the morale of the young man be her special care, or will
she let things slide?

But even articles like these were not the highpoint of success with
the *Express*, and before long Barbara was sent for by the proprietor
in person. Another crucial step in her romantic and professional
career had started.

Like several dozen better-looking and much younger men before
him, Lord Beaverbrook clearly fancied the young Barbara
Cartland, and he had more to tempt her with than all the

thoroughly nice young men she'd met till now. To start with he was a self-made millionaire. He owned the *Express* outright. He was dynamic, forceful and distinctly wicked. He was married, but like some bold Victorian seducer he told her that if she became his mistress he would set her up in luxury and make her the most famous female journalist in the world. To an ambitious modern miss in Fleet Street it must have seemed a tempting proposition – but not to Barbara.

Journalism made no difference to her principles nor to her purity. 'Besides,' she adds realistically, 'Max really seemed very, very old – although he was only just forty at the time – and I always had some exciting young man of about twenty-two in love with me all the time I knew him. How could I possibly consider him?'

It says much for the attractiveness of Barbara's personality that despite her firm refusal of the tycoon's dastardly suggestions, she still managed to retain his interest for a while. Throughout his life Beaverbrook enjoyed taking young journalists up to his mountain top, showing them the world beneath with all its riches – then dropping them. He did the same with Barbara – but the dropping did not come for quite some time.

Max always seemed extraordinarily interested in one from the start. He seemed to concentrate on one as if nothing else mattered, and I have never known anyone ask quite so many questions – where I had been, whom I had been with, what I had eaten, worn, thought, said and so on. It was exhausting but also rather flattering, especially as I never even kissed him. I was prudish and terribly religious at the time. I also had the sense to realise that nothing was more protective – especially for an older man – than innocence.

Although she was such a disappointment to his Lordship, he stuck to at least a part of his bargain, and while he failed to set her up in sinful luxury, he taught her something of the principles of journalism and writing for a popular mass-market. Beaverbrook never made her the greatest woman journalist in Britain, but it was his professional advice that ultimately helped her to become the most widely-read romantic novelist in the world.

For quite a while, Beaverbrook sub-edited and then personally rewrote every gossip item Barbara offered to the *Express*. It was an invaluable apprenticeship for a young ambitious writer, and he drummed into her the constant need for short sentences and direct and unadorned English. 'He gave me another key tip,' says Barbara. '"Never be boring." I remembered this many years later when I realised people listening incessantly to the radio and television always heard conversation. I then reduced all the paragraphs in my novels to about three lines – if they were longer the reader skipped them.'

Barbara was also most impressed by Max's extraordinary power of concentration – later she described it as being, 'what the Yogis call "point one concentration"' and she aspired to it herself. Another vital lesson that he taught her was the snob appeal the ancient aristocracy could still exert upon the newly literate mass readership, and he kept repeating the old Northcliffe adage, 'Get names into everything you write, and the more aristocratic the better.' Snobbery was an important selling point.

But perhaps the most important part of Beaverbrook's crash-course in the school of life, came when he introduced her to the circle of his private cronies. For a girl in her early twenties it was most exciting and something of an honour. As Barbara says, 'I was rather gay and bouncy in those days, and could generally make people laugh. Max used to send a car to take me to dinner at his little house in Roehampton, or take me down with him for a weekend at Cherkley, his country house. At both places I would find myself with celebrities like Lord Birkenhead, Lord Castlerosse and Winston Churchill.'

Luckily for Barbara, she insists that she has, 'never felt shy or suffered from nerves' – which was just as well in the company of the four most dominating men in Britain. 'I thought that what they wanted was a little wide-eyed girl who would listen to their stories and applaud and otherwise keep her mouth shut.'

This – for a while at least – she did, and for several months at this most impressionable period in Barbara's life, the Beaverbrook circle seems to have accepted her as something of a mascot. This did not interfere with her flourishing romantic escapades. After dinner at Roehampton there was usually some handsome young man waiting secretly with a car, round the corner from her house in London, to rush her off to dance at the Savoy. Max would have been furiously jealous if he had known.

But the Beaverbrook circle influenced Barbara rather more than she suspected at the time.

What struck me even then was that they were all so much more alive than any other group of men I'd ever seen before or since. They were always laughing. They weren't afraid of anyone, and their arguments seemed more passionate than any arguments I'd ever heard. They were always trying to cap each others' stories. Churchill would start off with some anecdote or other. The rest of them would shout, 'Winston, we've heard that one before,' and he'd reply, 'Well, Barbara hasn't,' and on he'd go.

Churchill had only just started painting as a hobby, and one afternoon at Cherkley, Barbara saw the great man seated at his easel, painting the view from the terrace.

'Why have you painted that bush purple?' she inquired pertly. 'It isn't purple.'

'It is to me – and that's what matters,' he growled back.

Lord Birkenhead performed his favourite party trick for her, of diving into the sea, at Cowes, with a lighted cigar between his lips, and surfacing with it still alight. Another member of the Beaverbrook circle, his great friend and fellow-Canadian, the millionaire financier, Sir James Dunn, proposed to her. But once again the doctrines of Miss Dell firmly prevented Barbara from accepting. She was not in love. Sir James was far too old and had been married. It was unthinkable. She gracefully declined.

But Barbara enjoyed the company of the piratical James Dunn, and it was through him she had her first real glimpse of the cosmopolitan fast set of the period, when he invited her to join a glittering party for a few days at the fashionable resort of Deauville. Despite his wealth and lavishness, it was not a success.

Dunn had rented Birkenhead's unsafe yacht, the *Mairi*, for the trip and as a gale was blowing in the Channel, Barbara, her best friend, the Marchioness of Queensberry, and the remainder of the party probably owed their lives to Lady Diana Cooper's very sensible insistence that they abandon ship and cross by the Channel ferry. Nöel Coward, fresh from the success of *London Calling*, joined the party at Deauville, but rain had set in, and neither Barbara's bounciness nor Coward's songs could raise morale.

Dunn, never able to resist a business deal, suggested an agreement to pay Nöel Coward £1,250 a year for the next five years in return for twenty per cent of everything he earned in the period. Coward finally declined, the rain continued, and when he said that Barbara was looking like 'Queen Gloom herself' at lunch she burst into tears. It was most unlike her.

One afternoon Barbara put her side curls in Hinde's pins and went to bed. She was asleep when a member of the party came into her bedroom to ask her to go to polo with them. They did not waken her and she said when she heard they had been: 'I must have looked awful!'

'Only very young,' was the answer.

It was this look which made men protective towards her. She was wandering about the casino, a little lost because most of the party had had too much to drink and she was teetotal, when an older man, good-looking and very rich whom she knew slightly came up to her and said: 'If you were my daughter I'd give you a good smacking and send you back to England!'

He took her back to her hotel and the next day proposed, but she refused him and the only bright spot in the disastrous little holiday came when James Dunn, having failed with Barbara, cut his losses and decided to elope with Lady Queensberry.

Altogether the week's holiday had proved Miss Dell's great point that money was not everything. But although Barbara kept her head – and her purity – and refused to fall in love with any of the buccaneers and millionaires around Lord Beaverbrook, their dominating characters undoubtedly impinged upon her own romantic aspirations at the time.

It was through Beaverbrook that Barbara met her first Duke. He was very tall, amazingly handsome with vivid blue eyes, fair hair and a Scot. He was a great landowner, very rich, very charming, aged thirty-five but – married! He fell very much in love with her but the gulf between them was unbridgeable. Barbara's idealised virginity made her refuse anything without marriage, while he was very much aware of his social and political importance. He asked Barbara to stay in one of his spendid fairytale houses, where the Duchess was coolly polite but his mother was very sweet and friendly. Love became friendship and he was to be one of Barbara's truest, most faithful and devoted friends all his life. His second wife is still adored by Barbara and all her family.

'The Duke, like all Max's friends,' she now recalls, 'seemed to me slightly unreal but fascinating, raffish, passionate and full of life.' Despite Miss Dell, there was a part of Barbara which was inevitably enamoured of them all, and although they never touched her, they did partially seduce her just the same.

Henceforth, her masculine ideal would always have a strong dash of Max Beaverbrook within it. Her ideal Duke would still be very grand, still young, still nobly and romantically good looking as Miss Dell had taught her that he had to be. But he would also have to be intelligent, a buccaneer, a touch sadistic, and something of a good red-blooded bounder. In those days Barbara still did not realise how unattainable such a man could be.

Not that she really had to worry. She was enjoying life. The

Twenties life of London was already in full swing, and Barbara was making the most of it with true Cartland gusto, still falling in and out of love with a succession of penniless and honourable young men, still turning down proposals left and right, still dancing until dawn, and still – incredible though it must seem today – preserving her virginity. 'In those days I did not even know what deep passionate kissing was,' she says. 'When I did learn many years later I was shocked.'

She became engaged – then disengaged. One suitor actually produced his officer's revolver in a taxi (an interesting period touch) and threatened to kill himself if she refused to marry him. Even this failed to sway her, and she relied increasingly on Polly now who had developed practised expertise in calming down her daughter's rejected suitors. The young man wept on Polly's shoulder, the threatened suicide did not take place, and Barbara bounced on through her early twenties, Park Gates and unwed Dukes apparently as far away as ever.

But in a way this hardly mattered, for Barbara had suddenly discovered her own private way of conjuring up the fine romantic world she wanted. Not long before she met Lord Beaverbrook, she had found herself at home during the summer holidays. Ronald was back from Charterhouse, revising for exams, and to give herself something to do she borrowed one of her brother's exercise books and began to write. The story rapidly rolled on. She had long been in the habit of telling herself romantic stories, and found little difficulty now in putting one down on paper. It was very Ethel M. Dell – but it was also very Barbara Cartland, full of the ambitions, dreams, excitements, risks that she had been living with for years.

Barbara had no secrets from Polly and naturally showed her the first few chapters. Somewhat typically, Polly insisted on showing them in turn to somebody whose opinion she could value – Lord Coventry's cousin Dick, who wrote verse for *Country Life*. He said to Barbara, 'It's interesting, finish it,' – and on she went.

The story was completed and dispatched on spec to Duckworth's, the publishers, who, most unusually for a first effort from a totally unknown novelist, accepted it on sight. And in March 1925 – on the same day incidentally that Duckworth's also published *Troy Park* by Edith Sitwell – Barbara's first novel duly appeared under the title *Jigsaw*. Almost overnight Barbara found herself slightly famous.

Barbara has always tended to belittle *Jigsaw*, but it remains extremely readable, and already demonstrates the author's considerable powers of driving, even breathless, narrative, and of creating a young heroine who convincingly embodies Barbara's own romantic dreams. Indeed, all the classic ingredients of a vintage Barbara Cartland are in *Jigsaw*, so it is worth a moment's brief examination, offering as it does a fascinating portrait of its youthful author and the dreams that she was living by.

The heroine, Mona Vivien, is clearly a self-portrait, romantically enhanced, of Barbara herself, a pert and fresh-complexioned virgin who, like the classic Cinderella heroine, finds herself suddenly in London fresh from boarding school. Instead of Netley Abbey, Mona has just left the devoted nuns of the Couvent du Sacré Cœur in Paris, France. Her grandmother, Countess Templedon, inhabits a romantic villa outside Florence, and Mona's father – just as Barbara's might conceivably have been had he survived the war – is a Conservative MP with a house in Belgrave Square.

One of the most attractive things about the book is the sense of sheer excitement which Barbara conveys of her first experience of London. 'The slight wind was whispering of adventures, excitements, fresh sensations, all palpitating, waiting to be discovered.' And Mona possesses 'the free joyous carelessness of untrammelled youth, still untouched by reality, her ideals as yet untarnished'.

Mona, like Barbara at the time, is terribly high-minded – and of course completely pure. 'She was absolutely ignorant of the heinous perversions of man. Vice was a word unknown in her vocabulary. Depraved jokes which the social world considered humorous were beyond her comprehension.' When her best friend is unfortunately seduced, Mona sees only, 'the pity of youth spilt like wine in the begriming dust, soiling its purity, besmirching white garments with the stains of uncleanness'.

But fortunately high ideals don't prevent Mona having her adventures – any more than they prevented Barbara. At a Mayfair party, Mona meets the inevitable tall, dark, handsome stranger, and as Barbara describes him, one sees instantly the unmistakable face of countless Cartland heroes for half a century to come. 'Dark hair was brushed from a broad brow, under which glinted two dark eyes, mocking and laughing intermittently. A firm mouth and jaw steadied the irresponsibility of the rest of the face. Attractively impertinent, he smiled back at her scrutiny.'

The owner of the mocking eyes suggests that he and Mona drive off through the night to see the sunrise, and with very little basis for such a rash assumption, Mona replies, 'I trust you'. He leads her to his nearby Mayfair mansion – in the hall an Irish wolf-hound is stretched out beside a brazier of alabaster – wraps her in choicest sables, and away they drive 'in a long car, shining like quickened mercury'.

Somewhere beyond Wimbledon they find a hillside and the dawn comes up. There is a chaste kiss on Mona's all-too-perfect lips and the two of them make a swift return to the party as if nothing much had happened.

A few weeks later, Mona finds her Duke, although to be strictly accurate, when he first appears he is a simple Marquis, Lord Peter Leadenhall, son and undoubted heir of the elderly Scottish Duke of Glenac. An Etonian, and a thorough gentleman, slim, rather puritanical, and just a little dull, he falls heavily in love with Mona. Mona though not bowled over, likes him : his manners and

his prospects do impress her and she marries him. The old Duke
dies, and suddenly she finds herself in the full splendour of the
Duchess of Glenac.

Then the trouble starts. Mona is introduced to her brother-in-
law, Alec, and discovers by the sort of blithe coincidence romantic
novelists delight in that he is none other than the dark young man
with the mocking eyes and the silver motor car, who once kissed
her in the dawn. Soon he suggests they should elope, and Mona is
distinctly tempted, although she is quite fond of Peter.

Peter was an impossible person to argue with. Arguments simply left
him unmoved, and he made allowances for her irritableness with a
disarming sweetness impossible to combat. If only he would lose his
temper, be brutal or abusive, Mona felt she would adore him. The
eternal considerateness and kindness towards her simply rasped on her
nerves. And yet she loved him; yes with the affection of a child for a
guardian. There was no passion for Peter the lover; there was no heart-
breaking thrill in their companionship.

It is an interesting analysis – and in its way it would come to be a
curiously prophetic one for Barbara. For throughout her life, there
have always been two sorts of men – the Alecs and the Peters. And
in *Jigsaw*, Mona finally rejects the bounder Alec, cleaves to the
sturdy Peter, and finally embarks on motherhood and happiness.

CHAPTER FOUR

The Wrong Man

An all-important part of Barbara's character – which has some-times caused misunderstanding in the press – has always been the contrast between the tender virgins in her novels, waiting to be cosseted, adored and doted on, and her dominating urge to work and to succeed. On the one hand she appears to be – and is – the most dedicated of professionals, who could give lessons to the Women's Liberation Movement on how a resourceful woman can achieve fame and financial independence by sheer hard work, becoming in the process rather more than the equal of any male around.

And on the other hand, there is the message of her books, and of her private life as well – the ideal she aspires to of the absolutely feminine woman, sexually distinctly shy, diffident before the all-important male in her life, devoted to her children, and engaged in making a shining shrine of womanhood before which devoted men will worship and reform themselves.

She herself is very conscious of this conflict, which has dogged her all her adult life. 'The truth is,' she admits, 'that there are really two quite separate "Mes". One is the crusader, who is impatient, rather aggressive, sometimes over-powerful, with a tendency to bulldoze everything before her. But at the same time, I have always had this other image of myself as a sort of flower-like creature, very delicate and feminine and always longing to be protected by a superior man. It is a sort of idealistic mental virginity, which I have given to my heroines – and which I've always had myself.'

This clash between the two quite separate Barbaras became

evident during her period of success after writing *Jigsaw*. The
book had short, but reasonably flattering reviews. 'When she takes
courage to profit from her mistakes,' pontificated the *Inquirer*, 'she
ought to win a respectable place among our rising novelists.'
There were six editions, five separate translations, and although
Jigsaw failed to make her rich, it did make her something of a
celebrity at twenty-four. Today this rather puzzles her. 'It seems
funny now to remember what a lot of attention was paid to a first
novel without much distinction or literary quality, but its value
from a publicity point of view lay in the fact that it was a social
story written by a girl with a social background.'

For the reviewers and the writers in the popular dailies, took
Barbara's dream at its face value, treating her as if she were, like
Mona Vivien, married to a Duke. *Jigsaw* was widely publicised as
the story of 'Mayfair from Within' or still more promising,
'Mayfair With the Lid Off'. Barbara herself, 'an extremely
charming young lady, said to be one of the most graceful dancers
in Mayfair', was somewhat breathlessly described as, 'pure Saxon
in type and very proud to be able to trace her ancestry back to the
thirteenth century'. She was even criticised as if Mayfair had
suddenly become her very own responsibility. 'If this is Mayfair,'
the *News Chronicle* exclaimed, 'then let me live in Whitechapel.'

As well as the social cachet, *Jigsaw* – and its authoress – also
benefited from the extraordinary impression that it, and she, were
somehow 'fast'. One of her Scobell aunts declared that Barbara
had been 'tarnished' by her new-found notoriety. This impression
that there was something slightly fast about Barbara Cartland
was increased when she wrote a play, entitled *Blood Money*, which
was promptly banned by the Lord Chamberlain himself. In fact the
banning of the play had no connection with its morals – or the lack
of them. The good Lord Chamberlain was simply worried that
Barbara had inadvertently used the names of two living members
of the House of Lords – an unspeakable offence – and this was
rapidly corrected.

Blood Money failed to repeat the success of *Jigsaw*. It played for
several weeks to mixed reviews at the old Q Theatre which used to
be by Kew Bridge, but it failed to reach Shaftesbury Avenue.
Totally undaunted, and patently enjoying her publicity, Barbara
was driving on with all her mother's energy. Soon she was
composing both the book and lyrics for a charity performance of
the 'Mayfair Review' which was staged at the Hotel Cecil with the
Duchess of Rutland and the Marchioness of Ely among its eminent
Vice-Presidents.

She was still writing social snippets for the press, and helping
other young people to succeed, including a young Cambridge
undergraduate called Norman Hartnell. She was his first custo-
mer, at a very reduced price, and in return she persuaded many of
her rich friends to patronise him.

Blood Money was rapidly revamped into a novel which she
entitled *Sawdust*, and Barbara also found time to follow Polly's
knitwear shop with a hat shop called, inevitably, 'Barbara'.

Even this was news. 'Sixteen hours a day. Society shopkeeper
finds work agrees with her,' marvelled the *Evening Standard*.

But the hat shop proved too much — even for Barbara — for she
was still leading her determined double-life as a romantic virgin,
still dancing every night with adoring young men, and still on the
lookout for that increasingly unattainable young man who
would combine the romantic splendour of a Duke, the looks of a
hero out of Elinor Glyn, and the driving personality of Lord
Beaverbrook. Small wonder that it took her quite some time to
find him.

What with her blossoming reputation — and so much energy, good
looks and high ambitions and ideals — Barbara was rather a
formidable young lady now. A surviving admirer from this period
— now a retired army Major living quietly in Hampshire —
remembers her as, 'terribly stylish and pretty, don't you know, but
far too clever for the likes of me'.

Despite, or possibly because of this, the manic tempo of her love affairs was showing signs of getting out of hand. When one says 'love affairs', the term is still used in the romantic, not the modern sense, but there was no guarantee that her high-mindedness would last. Just before *Blood Money* was staged, Barbara had been on the edge of the unthinkable – marriage with a man already married who was prepared to have a divorce because he was in love with her. He was tall, dark, handsome, very rich and was, she says, 'considerably attractive'. He was, however, so in love and so bemused by Barbara's idealism, he never even suggested a more irregular relationship.

As usual Barbara discussed it all with Polly who was horrified at the idea of her 'breaking a marriage'. To Polly, marriage blessed by God was for life! There was also the distraction offered by her play – and Barbara was saved. Later she ruefully admitted that she had probably been 'playing at being in love'. Just the same it could have been unfortunate. There was also an aristocratic actor who proposed and pursued her passionately. Barbara was thrilled with his family tree, loved his relatives and their ancestral homes but thought the stage life very narrow and restrictive and felt it was not for her.

A few months later, she was still more deeply involved with a young naval officer. 'He was a wonderful dancer, which was most important in those days, and it was very very physical. To tell the truth, I was a little frightened by it all, and felt it would be wrong to marry him simply for that.'

Perhaps it would have been. At all events, by Christmas 1926, Barbara had reached the point of feeling that her life must be resolved. She had been keeping scrupulous account of the marriage proposals she had had. The naval officer, as honourable as all the rest, had made it forty-eight – which was flattering, but also rather worrying. How much longer could she possibly go on turning young men down?

She admits that suddenly she felt as if her life had become 'empty and frivolous', and it was time she pulled herself together and became more serious.

The forty-ninth proposal duly came along, and prompted by the fact that she was not particularly well – and by her new decisive mood – she suddenly accepted. The driving, energetic Barbara had finally surrendered to the Barbara of the pedestal, waiting quietly to be cosseted and loved.

The lucky man was twenty-nine-year-old Alexander McCorquodale. He was not a Duke – nor had he even got a title. But the McCorquodales were very rich and Scottish. As *Jigsaw* showed, Barbara had always found the Scots romantic. The family had made a fortune as printers for the Government – they produced all the postal orders at the time – and although Alexander could not yet boast Park Gates of his own, his parents lived in an impressive Queen Anne mansion, Cound (pronounced 'Coon') Hall, Shropshire.

Alexander seemed a good approximation to a Cartland hero, having considerable charm, dark, slightly brooding Scottish looks, a silent manner, which to Barbara always promised depths of hidden passion, and he patently adored her. He also seemed to have considerable knowledge of the world – and women – was an accomplished salmon fisherman and a very fine game shot.

Polly who, for some time now, had been concerned at Barbara's unwillingness to settle down, was delighted at the prospect of her marriage, although she did have reservations at her daughter's choice. 'Is he really *worthy* of you darling?' she inquired. Barbara replied she thought he was.

She admitted that her future in-laws were not particularly exciting, but Alexander was rather different. Besides, he had promised her a house in Mayfair and her own Rolls-Royce.

But did she really love him? wise old Polly asked.

'Of course,' said Barbara quickly, knowing in her heart of hearts she wasn't *wildly* in love. But perhaps that was because she was tired and was expecting too much too quickly. She was sure it would be all right. Elinor Glyn's heroines always married and lived happily ever after. So would she. 'I was quite determined I would be a wonderful, wonderful wife,' says Barbara.

It was a true Barbara Cartland wedding on St George's Day in April: St Margaret's Westminster, a bevy of child bridesmaids in pink, a Bishop to conduct the ceremony and Barbara herself quite radiant in what she claims was the first full-scale tulle wedding-dress worn in London since the war. It had been designed for her as a wedding present by Norman Hartnell.

The bridesmaids' dresses were copied from a shaded pink evening dress which Barbara had bought at a second-hand clothes shop from which she bought the majority of her dresses. It had belonged to Mrs Dudley Ward, who was the acknowledged mistress of the Prince of Wales.

Barbara and Alexander's honeymoon should have been very romantic. They planned to motor 5,000 miles round Europe in their brand-new black-and-white Rolls, and visit the most perfect places – Cannes, Florence, Venice, the Italian Lakes. But during the trip Barbara cried a lot and discovered she had septic tonsils. Back in England she was forced to spend some weeks in bed where she read Trollope and Jane Austen before an operation.

Perhaps it was Miss Austen's astringent influence after so much Elinor Glyn, or perhaps it was the septic tonsils. Perhaps Barbara had been prizing and protecting her virginity so long that its surrender, in the midst of all that frantic motoring, had been something of an anti-climax. Whatever the true cause the fact remained that Barbara was, though she would not admit it even to herself, disappointed.

Ethel M. Dell had convinced her that when men, and particularly Scots, were strong and silent, they were naturally pulsating with dark hidden passion. Not so Alexander. He was just strong and very silent. And although he treated Barbara with considerable solicitude and care, the romantic Barbara could not help feeling that he had failed to sweep her off her feet, as she had expected.

Some years later Barbara perhaps analysed what had really happened in a short article on marriage which she contributed to the *Evening News*.

Let me tell you about a friend of mine we will call Belinda . . . Belinda was impulsive, generous, gay, with an able intelligence which would develop with age. She was incurably romantic, having been brought up on a mixture of fairy stories and historical novels, and like many a young girl before her, she was attracted by what she did not understand. Her male counterpart was one of the young men she had danced, swum and chattered with since she was a schoolgirl. She understood them, shared their ambitions, their joys and disappointments. The only thing they lacked for her was the 'unknown'.

She dreamed of a strong silent cave-man – a man of deeds but of few words – a man who underneath a deep reserve was passionate, commanding, conquering. Finally she thought that she had found him in her husband. She mistook inertia for reserve, lack of interest for silent strength and indifference for hidden passion. She was bitterly, miserably disappointed. She had married the wrong man.

For a while Barbara tried desperately to make her marriage work. First came a trip to Norway in the summer *en famille* with Alexander and his parents in the big yacht which they had rented at considerable expense. Barbara didn't care for Norway (she had been hoping for the South of France), nor the cold, nor the sea. But she did enjoy the Orkneys, and she and her husband decided to have a house there. Back in London there was the excitement of setting up home in Mayfair – something she had set her heart on.

Soon the society magazines were cooing over the new arrival on the social scene.

Mrs Alexander McCorquodale (the novelist, Barbara Cartland) has a delightful little house in Culross Street, Park Lane, where the decorations and the furniture are very up-to-date. The bath is a gay affair of orange, and the prevailing colour in the house is jade green. There is a fine old Spanish four-poster in the master bedroom.

In the *Tatler* there was a photograph of a wistful-looking Barbara and the announcement that, 'Mrs McCorquodale, an accomplished hostess, will be one of London's leading social figures this season.'

She duly was. Alexander had a large income and his parents had £50,000 a year. The little house in Culross Street was soon humming with activity as the energetic Barbara once again took over from the romantic one. A new novel — it would be her third — was on the stocks, and Barbara was now attempting to fulfil that youthful promise she had made to Ronald about 'getting to know everyone in London.' But here again, her husband proved a disappointment. Despite his prowess on the grouse moor and the salmon river, he was not happy in the jade green drawing-room, and Barbara began to think he suffered from that most insidious of social diseases — inverted snobbery.

It was unfortunate, but even that was not fatal to the marriage — yet. For at the beginning of 1928 the great moment Barbara had dreamed of duly came. She found that she was pregnant.

An important part of her philosophy has always been the importance of a mother to her child. As she has said,

I think a mother influences her child from the very moment of conception. I think too that how it is conceived is of paramount importance. If the union of spiritual and physical love evokes in the act of conception the ecstasy which is as near as we get to the Divine — then the child will be beautiful.

Barbara was thrilled! This was what she had always wanted and prayed for since she got married. Now she was going to make sure her child was perfect.

When I was carrying my daughter, I was determined she should be beautiful, and I not only looked at Beauty but thought it. I would never read a book or watch a film which I thought could induce in me wrong or bad thoughts and might affect my unborn child.

Convinced of the influence of the mother's state of mind upon her unborn child, she even placed a picture of her ideal baby near her bed. That September, when the birth occurred, Barbara was delighted to observe how similar her baby was to the picture she had been gazing on for months. 'My first visitors saw it and as the resemblance was so extraordinary they exclaimed, "You had her painted already!"'

The romantic novelist in Barbara was determined that her daughter should have a name as beautiful, and original, as one of her own heroines. She chose the Gaelic name of Raine, and almost from the moment of her birth Raine McCorquodale was news. The *Daily Sketch* was currently conducting a silly-season weighing-in of top society babies. Raine came number two.

(1) Lady Alington's Mary	9 lb 4 oz
(2) Mrs McCorquodale's Raine	7 lb 10¾ oz
(3) Lady Diana Cooper's Julius	7 lb 4 oz
(4) Princess Bismarck's daughter	7 lb 5 oz

Two days later *The Lady* was reporting Raine's first party.

The christening of Raine McCorquodale at St Margaret's by the Bishop of Chelmsford was followed by a very gay party indeed at the McCorquodales' house in Culross Street where, as usual, there were leaping flames on the hearth and flowers everywhere. Dozens of young men come to christening parties now and try to say the right thing about the baby. Mrs McCorquodale has one of the nicest brothers in the world, who is very keen on politics and working in settlements.

Instead of bringing the parents closer together, Raine's birth marked the beginning of a round of fresh activity for Barbara, and just a few weeks later the indefatigable social reporter in the *Daily Sketch* was speculating that, 'Barbara Cartland (Mrs Alexander McCorquodale) must surely be one of the busiest women in

London'. For apart from looking after baby Raine, writing another novel, and 'entertaining friends almost every afternoon',

she is an *active* organiser of the matinée at the Prince of Wales Theatre on December 3 in aid of two Thames-side settlements; the Orange Grove Ball on December 4 at the Hyde Park Hotel in aid of the St Cecilia's Children's Clinic; the special appeal for the Save the Children's Fund on December 11; the 3 Arts Club Ball on December 17 at Grosvenor House; a tea party at the May Fair Hotel, at which the Prime Minister will speak; and the Empress Cabaret and Santa Claus Ball on December 18 at the Kit-Cat Club in aid of Queen Charlotte's Hospital.

And so the merry round progressed, with Barbara soon as occupied as she had been before her marriage, entertaining and organising affairs for charity. Just a few weeks after Raine was born, Barbara had found herself a fresh activity, delivering six weekly radio talks on the general subject of 'Making the Best of Oneself'.

One of the many useful lessons Barbara had picked up from Beaverbrook had been the need for what he called a 'platform', by which he meant a set of beliefs by which a politician or a public figure becomes known to everyone. Barbara had never been afraid of airing her opinions and now she made the most of them. Femininity and self-improvement became *her* platform, and she was soon suggesting ways in which her female listeners could improve their lives and generally cheer up those around them.

They should express themselves within their homes, she said, by painting their rooms bright colours just as she had done. They should learn proper relaxation, take more care about their diet, study their dress and makeup. As the *Radio Times* said in its issue for the New Year, 1929,

Barbara Cartland introduces a new and most attractive theory. Her idea is largely to do good to others by doing good to oneself. It is possible, by putting on a pretty dress or making up one's face to confer a good deal more gladness in the New Year than by stopping smoking or getting up early in the morning. This doctrine should appeal to all our women listeners.

But the way that Barbara made the most of *herself* now was really through her energy and organising skill. What with her talks, her novels and her Mayfair parties she was becoming a celebrity and she increasingly involved herself in running the full-scale charity affairs which kept society amused as the Twenties ended.

As a former Beaverbrook social gossip writer, and the author of 'Mayfair with the Lid Off', Barbara had few illusions about London's smart 'Society' – or about the snobbery, ambition, hunger for publicity and general silliness which kept so much of the city's 'Vanity Fair' in motion. Still less did she believe 'Society' was smitten with a longing for good works or an impelling generosity towards the poor. As she has written of this period,

Charity had become a ladder with which to climb the social tree. Organisers looked round for rich women who were socially ambitious. They accepted the chairmanship of a charity performance and met the Royal Patrons and the distinguished Vice-Presidents. They paid through the nose for the privilege.

Barbara had no money of her own to give to charity if she had wanted to, but it amused her to exploit the undeserving rich. Besides, as she admits, 'it kept me out of mischief' at a time when she was increasingly worried about her marriage.

She was seeing less and less of Alexander now and towards the end of 1929 it had been Barbara's bright idea to enhance the dinner-dance at the Kit-Cat Club, in aid of Queen Charlotte's Hospital, by making it a full-scale 'Queen Charlotte's Birthday Dinner' complete with a pageant of spectacularly-dressed society ladies. For once again she was remembering Northcliffe's adage about 'names and the more aristocratic the better'.

Lady Dunn – the former Marchioness of Queensberry, who after a number of difficulties and divorces was now married to Sir

James – came dressed up as 'White Wine', Lady Castlerosse was
the 'Fish Course', Lady Scarsdale the 'Goose', and Barbara herself
made her appearance appropriately as 'Champagne', in a specially
concocted dress of golden tissue wrapped in yards and yards of a
new material called celophane. Lady Curzon turned down the part
of 'Queen Charlotte' on the grounds that Charlotte was 'such a
very ugly woman', and the queenly part was played by Binnie
Hale.

For Barbara this performance marked the beginning of a series
of full-scale social pageants which she organised with great success.
There was a Railway Ball at Covent Garden, with famous beauties
representing famous trains; the Superstitions Ball, the Looking
Glass Ball, a Guy Fawkes Conspiracy Party and she also took part
in the Jewel Ball, at the Dorchester Hotel, in which several
million pounds' worth of precious stones were worn in the parade.

But Barbara's triumph was undoubtedly the pageant she
produced and designed in the vast acreage of the Royal Albert Hall
on the unlikely-sounding theme of Britain and her Industries. The
dresses had to be immense. Lady Ashley in black sequined tights
came on as 'Coal', with a black oilcloth train thirty yards square
behind her; Lady Scarsdale came as 'Wool' in a massive woollen
crinoline; Lily Elsie was Britannia; and Barbara stole the show.
'My own dress, given by the White Star Line, and shared by three
attendants, was a huge, canvas-covered trolley painted to look like
the sea, and bearing on its white crested waves a model liner lit up
in every porthole.'

After the pageant, when she had shed her liner, Barbara had her
due reward. The heir to the throne was present in the Royal Box.
She met him, was congratulated by him, and became one of the
envied ladies of the period who had genuinely 'danced with the
Prince of Wales'.

That boast which she had made to Ronald just a few years earlier
about 'getting to know everyone in London' was coming true. But
was she happy?

She should have been, for as her twenties drew towards their close it seemed that she had managed to achieve most of the worldly aims which the ambitious side of her had wanted. After those almost fatal setbacks to her parents' fortunes, she was established with a gathering of titled friends, a Rolls-Royce and a house in Mayfair.

She thoroughly enjoyed her new-found affluence, being able to entertain, and was rarely out of the society papers. Her novels got her talked about and her work as a sort of social impresario – the papers called her 'the C.B. Cochran of amateurs' – had even given her considerable social influence. She had her daughter and was devoted to her; she dressed elegantly; and at the end of 1929 she managed to persuade her husband to take her off on the sort of holiday she had always dreamed of. Instead of frozen Norway with the elderly McCorquodales, they journeyed up the Nile, stayed for a while in Luxor – 'the Winter Palace had the hardest beds and best gin fizzes we met anywhere' – then stopped off in Monte Carlo where she even had beginner's luck at the casino.

She had been praying that the holiday would somehow bring her closer to her husband and as she says, they had done all the 'right' things, but as it turned out there was little chance of that by now, and she returned to London trying not to admit what she had really known for many months: that her marriage was a failure. She did not however give in, and was determined to go on fighting as Polly had fought and won.

But now there was something more than her early disappointment with Alexander as a lover. Time and affection might have overcome such failings, but she learnt that he had a weakness which was an overwhelming shock.

She had already written about it in a novel which she had published earlier that year under the title *If the Tree be Saved*. The heroine Tain McSpean, another of Barbara's Scottish Cinderellas, is a romantic, very pretty orphan who, like Mona Vivien, arrives in

London fresh from school and marries the wealthy, charming Jimmy Oakley, heir to an ancient title and a stately home. But the marriage, just like Barbara's, is a disappointment. For all his charm, Jimmy is a useless husband and after several months of puzzled tears, the heroine discovers why. Jimmy is a secret drinker, and there is no mistaking the depth of feeling with which Barbara put the case against him.

A blackguard, a fornicator, thief, villain, even cad, can all be managed by a woman, but a man who drinks, living only for the moment in a hazy, distorted world of his own, is unapproachable. . . . So Tain looked at her husband and saw a man she did not know.

Barbara in 1923

The Down House, Redmarley, Polly's home which has been the background of so many of Barbara's novels

Polly and Bertie when they were engaged in 1899

Polly's wedding in 1900

Barbara aged 11 months with her Nanny and Rags in 1901

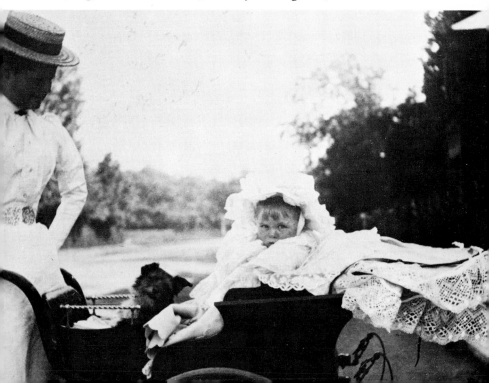

Ronald and Barbara in 1908

'The Little Slide', Barbara's first book. She wrote, bound and illustrated it herself when she was five

once upon a time
there was a little girl
and her name
was Mary
now this little
girl was very
found of making

Polly, Barbara and Ronald in 1909

Barbara's wedding to Alexander McCorquodale on St George's Day, 23 April 1927. Among the bridesmaids were the daughters of the Marquis of Queensbury, Viscount Scarsdale, Viscount Monsell, Lady Domville and Zena Dare

RIGHT Barbara with her first child, Raine, in 1929. This was acclaimed as a perfect mother and child picture

Barbara (*right*) with the Hon. Mrs Cunningham-Reid, a close and loyal friend

Barbara with her glider which carried the first glider air mail from London to Reading in 1931. An aeroplane-towed glider was the original idea of Barbara and two young Air-Force officers

CHAPTER FIVE

The Undaunted Divorcee

At Camfield Place Barbara sleeps in a resplendent scarlet and gold antique four-poster with a gilded angel, wings outspread, high above the bed-head. He is a reminder, she insists, of the ups-and-downs which have afflicted her throughout her life.

Nothing has ever been easy, and I've generally had a long hard battle to get what I wanted. Seeing me today, few people realise what a struggle life has been at times, but like all my family I'm a born survivor, and I enjoy having something positive to fight against. When my marriage ended, I was wretchedly unhappy for a time, but I had to fight and that was good for me. In different ways I've been fighting ever since.

This is the voice of hindsight, and Barbara had no way of knowing quite how grim a future lay around the corner when by 1930 she accepted that her marriage to Alexander was in ruins. To the outside world – and to the countless friends and smart acquaintances who flocked to the little house in Culross Street – she was still the most enviable of women. There was no let-up in the frantic social round and her pioneering spirit kept her firmly in the news.

That May she was busy organising a full-scale motor-rally with Lord Donegall at Bray, and had persuaded Malcolm Campbell and Tim Birkin to act as judges. Later she even drove at Brooklands in a supercharged MG as the organiser and one of the competitors in the first ladies motor-race.

But after that marathon honeymoon drive with Alexander, nothing could make her an enthusiastic motorist, and like a truly modern woman of her times she was soon trying aeroplanes. For a while she was an enthusiastic flier, and if her life had turned out differently she might well have joined the ranks of record-breaking female fliers of the Thirties. As it was she became intrigued by the latest possibilities of gliding and her own glider – the newly built 'Barbara Cartland' – was towed from Manston to Reading carrying mail, the first aeroplane-towed glider-borne mail in history.

It was all very dashing, very up-to-date, and brought her the publicity she still enjoyed, and which helped to sell her books. Her romantic life had suddenly become happy too, for she was in love. Since they returned from Egypt, she and Alexander had been leading virtually separate lives, but on a trip to Paris he had introduced her to a man who could easily have been one of the heroes from her novels. Tall, dark and something of a lady-killer, Commander Glen Kidston was the sort of man that Alexander failed to be. Debonair, rich, self-assured, he lived dangerously, piloting his own plane, restlessly travelling the globe and making no secret of his amorous conquests.

They danced, they met at parties, and they were powerfully attracted to each other. But at the same time Barbara was still something of the 'wise virgin' she had been before her marriage. She realised the danger of a scandal. She knew that she was vulnerable, and was wary of risking everything for him.

Then came tragedy. Kidston had bought the aeroplane from which Alfred Lowenstein, the Belgian financier, had fallen to his death over the English Channel. Barbara hated it and thought the plane ill-omened, but Kidston laughed at her fears and told her he intended to test-fly the plane to South Africa. She pleaded with him not to, but he was adamant, and on a misty cold spring morning, early in 1931, she drove to Croydon Airport to see him off. She never saw him again and soon after news came through that his aeroplane had hit a hillside. His body was brought back to Wales for burial – and Barbara's photographs were found with his effects.

As if this was not enough, less than a year later she discovered that Alexander was in love – with Glen Kidston's sister, Eleanor. And with appalling irony, it was because of this that she was abruptly dragged into the pitched battle of a no-holds-barred divorce.

When she had found a batch of letters written by Eleanor to Alexander, Barbara's immediate reaction had been to offer him a swift divorce, but it was not to be that simple. Part of the trouble was quite simply money. Alexander, and his lawyers, were afraid of the heavy damages he would have to pay if she divorced him as the guilty party to an undefended suit. More serious still was the vexed question of the custody of Raine. Not unnaturally, Barbara had no intention of relinquishing her only daughter. Nor had Alexander – if he could help it. His family supported him, his lawyers scenting the rich pickings of a big society divorce encouraged him, and the battle started.

The first that Barbara knew of what was going on, came one evening when her brother Ronald called for her and spotted a man on the opposite side of the street obviously watching the house. Quite casually he asked him who he was, and the man confided that he was a private detective. Ronald made inquiries and the truth came out. Alexander and his lawyers were attempting to grub up evidence in the hope of suing Barbara for divorce. So desperate were they that for a while Ronald was included in the case against Barbara as an 'unidentified' male caller. And to show that they meant business they hurriedly briefed one of the most eminent – and expensive – barristers in the country, the formidable Sir Norman Birkett.

For Barbara this was dreadful news. She had a foolproof case, but she had no funds to hire a barrister of the calibre of Birkett to defend her. She was vulnerable and suddenly her prospects looked distinctly grim.

But one of Ronald's girl-friends at the time was Barbara Hastings, daughter of the famous barrister and playwright, Sir Patrick Hastings. Ronald mentioned to him what was happening, and he was instantly outraged. It was blatantly unfair, he thundered. The McCorquodales were simply using their money and hiring a famous attorney to enable a rich guilty husband to take advantage of his wife, avoid paying alimony he could well afford, and gain custody of Raine. If Birkett represented Alexander, he would do the same for Barbara – for nothing.

The case came up for trial in the autumn of 1932, with both sides suing for divorce, and it inevitably hit the headlines. Hastings and Birkett were both legal *prima donnas*, Barbara was something of a celebrity, and the case was just the sort the papers loved. A lot of mud was thrown in public, and an awful lot of Alexander's money went to his lawyers as the case dragged on.

It was distinctly futile, for Barbara, as one might expect, was an unshakeable witness in the box. Since Alexander's solicitors asked for a jury, thinking they would disapprove of Barbara's looks and publicity, Ronald made her appear in Court in a simple black dress wearing very little makeup and no nail varnish, which was still considered rather fast. In contrast, Alexander was an unimpressive witness, frequently confused and contradicting himself. Neither the judge nor the jury was impressed and he lost the case. Barbara was awarded her divorce, with costs and custody of Raine.

She was vindicated – but she was also all but ruined. For the expense of the case had been enormous to her former husband, since the wretched man was also being sued by Eleanor's husband as a direct result of the divorce. All his personal fortune had to go in settling the costs, and although his parents gave him a huge allowance to support himself, Barbara had nothing except the marriage settlement. Their house was sold, and so was the Rolls-Royce.

Just a few weeks before, she had been a rich and envied social figure with a host of friends, success and almost everything that she could want from life. Overnight everything had changed. Now she had nothing except a delicate child, £500 a year, and the social stigma of a widely publicised divorce. As she has said: 'It was a useful test of who my real friends would be.'

Polly, as one might have predicted, was magnificent. Although she was very upset, there was no reproach for what had happened. For a few weeks Barbara, now without a house, was living in the Dorchester at a pound a night, and eating all her meals with friends. Then Polly found her what she needed — a maisonette in Half Moon Street for seven pounds a week. It seemed somewhat small but the spare bedrooms could be turned into nurseries for Raine. And although not knowing where the next month's rent was coming from, Barbara was still living where she intended to — in Mayfair.

This was typical of her. 'Part of my philosophy of life,' she says, 'is never to admit that you've been beaten or done down. The moment you do that, you've lost. Quite early on I learned that the best way to survive is to pretend that anything unpleasant simply hasn't happened.'

She did her best to do this now, although it took a major exercise of will to pretend that life was still as rosy and benign as it had been six months before. Reading between the lines one gets a clear impression of an indomitable Barbara, colourful as ever in her new surroundings. In a gushing article on 'Other People's Homes', a *Glasgow Evening News* reporter wrote soon after the divorce:

Another exquisite bedroom is that of Mrs Alexander McCorquodale, who has, in common with many other Society matrons, moved out of her big house in Mayfair into a much smaller one in Half Moon St. which was originally intended for a bachelor's dwelling. Her bedroom has walls of vivid turquoise blue and her four-poster is covered with flame-coloured brocade. The bath-dressing room next door is a delicious affair of jade-green and rose. . . . Small though the house is, Mrs McCorquodale by careful planning, has even managed a nursery suite for her daughter Raine, out of what were formerly the valet's apartments.

It was all very similar to the way Polly had survived thirty years before when disaster struck the Cartland fortune. And just like Polly, Barbara, whilst keeping up those precious 'standards' she believed in, was all set to fight to earn herself a living.

It was, she now admits, 'a time of deep unhappiness, when the whole world seemed dark and frightening', but she adds that it simply was not in her nature to sit around and cry, 'Poor little me! I decided I would go in with fists flying.' And she did.

Luckily she had her training as a journalist and publicist, and still enjoyed her reputation as the impresario of the pageants and the charity affairs that she had staged. Also the novel that she published on the eve of her divorce – it was entitled irresistibly, *A Virgin in Mayfair* – had been a well-deserved success, and as with *Jigsaw* made her name as one of the few accredited social figures who were prepared to tell the world what really happened in 'Society'. This curious obsession with the doings, and the indiscretions of the titled, powerful and rich (most of whom, in fact, were rather staid and boring) was at its height, thanks to the revelations and the steady stream of gossip churned out in the daily press. And Barbara, quite sensibly, made the most of it.

At a time when Duchesses were queuing up to advertise cold cream, one of Barbara's first successes was a blood-curdling series in the *Passing Show* on the 'Secrets of Society'. The first was on the fascinating subject of 'Black Masses in Mayfair' – 'In Mayfair there are a few, just a few rich people who have discovered and shamelessly revel in the weird fascination of magic.'

A second on the subject of 'Paid Hostesses' revealed that although it is a thankless task, 'more and more impoverished women of title are trying to make a profession and a living from it'. And her most intriguing revelation of all was on the unpleasant subject of 'Freak Parties'.

' There is a definite canker in the heart of Mayfair known as the freak party . . . which are not only exhibitions of vulgarity, but also orgies of indecency and drunkenness. . . . Imagine a large room. The host is magnificently attired as a music-hall dancer of the 1890s, his wig is a work of art, so are his underclothes and high-heeled shoes. His shoulders, revealed by the low-cut dress, are powdered and his face is well made-up, even to the black patch on his rouged cheeks. . . . It is noticeable that most men are dressed as women and that they prefer to dance together.

Perhaps there is rather more of the imaginative novelist than the professional reporter in these articles, but they helped pay the bills and build her name up as a journalist. And during these first few crucial months of living on her own, Barbara's real success came from her instinctive flair for publicity.

All that activity for charity was now an invaluable apprenticeship – so was her training from Lord Beaverbrook and the sort of help she had given Norman Hartnell. For better than almost anyone, Barbara understood the power of famous names and how to use them. Just as with her early journalism it was 'names and the more aristocratic the better', and she made something of a speciality of what she called 'psychology publicity'. She explained it with disarming candour :

Advertisement no longer meant spending money in the advertisement columns of the newspapers. The gossip columns were the best and surest medium of attraction as far as the London area was concerned, for social names were the surest bait to catch the wealthy suburban worm. The suburbs really seemed to be the only people who have paid in full for everything everywhere and they paid heavily for their snobbery.

She was in fact one of the very first to grasp the publicity potential of the ever-expanding popular press, and skilfully exploited it.

One of her first coups was to put the Westminster Ice Rink on the social map, by organising gala nights, and making sure the press was there to report the presence, and the antics, of her specially invited guests. Still more successful was her work with the once fashionable but now declining Embassy Club. Here famous names alone were not enough to revive its flagging fortunes, and it was Barbara who totally revamped the image of the club.

She did this with her own inimitable mixture of realism and romance, grasping the point at once that those who make or break a smart expensive nightclub like the Embassy are the well-to-do, 'who are usually getting on in life but are seeking romance. They want to feel glamorous, to imagine themselves in love, if only for the evening.' They could not do this in the harshly-lit Twenties decor of the club as it was when the Prince of Wales had made it famous ten years earlier. Instead she persuaded the management to, 'let me do the whole place up rather like my bedroom, with Nile blue walls, a coral carpet and orange-pink lighting which was very flattering and romantic'.

Once again Barbara was right, and she had the bright idea of offering free food and charging well for the drinks, where the real profits lay. The Embassy began to boom again, especially with Barbara bringing countless celebrities and friends to get it mentioned in the press.

She had a natural ingenuity at getting places talked about and rarely failed. One somewhat staid West End dressmaker she took on, trebled its clientele as soon as Barbara started introducing important society customers – and making sure that they were mentioned in the gossip columns. And when her old admirer, Sir James Dunn, invested in an 'Instant Cleaning' business, Barbara took charge of that as well. Once again the Cartland formula brought quick results. Her idea here was to offer a quicker cleaning service than anywhere else in London, and to get the shop talked about by having the cleaning gift-wrapped in yellow paper with a bright pink bow.

It seemed that she was always rushing, always on the go, and her only big mistake was in usually working for an outright fee – never for a share of the profits she brought in. Because of this, money – or the lack of it – remained a constant problem, with Barbara needing all her cleverness and mother wit to meet the expenses of the flat in Half Moon Street and to ensure she lived the life that she had set her heart on.

And what exactly was that life, now that she found herself a single woman, her thirtieth birthday rapidly approaching, and living with a year-old daughter in the heart of London?

Over one important detail she was fortunate. The McCorquodales agreed to pay for a Nanny for Raine, thus leaving Barbara free to work. She was also lucky with a few extremely faithful friends. On the whole Barbara has never particularly enjoyed the company of women – nor does she have a high regard for them as friends. As she has candidly admitted.

I have always found women difficult. I don't really understand them. To begin with, few women tell the truth. I always say what I think and feel – it's got me into trouble, but only with women. I've never had a cross word with a man for speaking frankly, but women don't like it. I can't think why unless it's natural love of subterfuge and intrigue.

But there were one or two exceptions. One of course was Polly, who remained the loyalest of allies and most unshockable of confidantes. And another was a red-haired, newly married heiress she had recently met at a party given by the future owner of *Picture Post*, Edward Hulton.

Mary Cunningham-Reid had started life as Mary Ashley, sister of Edwina Ashley, (who in 1922 would marry Lord Louis Mountbatten in the most glittering wedding of the Season). As a granddaughter of the great Edwardian financier, Sir Ernest Cassel, Mary was invariably described by the press as 'the £80,000 a year heiress'. Polly had met her in the war when she stayed at Broadlands with Bertie, and had told Barbara that, unlike her older sister, Mary had seemed 'rather sad and shy'. She was still shy when Barbara met her, and Barbara saw her as something of a 'prisoner in a glittering golden cage fashioned by money, and limelit by publicity'.

No one could have been more different from the gregarious, unsinkable, limelight-loving Barbara. There was the inevitable attraction of opposites, and they rapidly became devoted friends, which they have remained to this day. For Mary, Barbara was a life-enhancer, a continual source of fun and someone she could turn to for advice through all the tribulations of her stormy marriage to the unscrupulous Cunningham-Reid. And for Barbara this new friend was even more important, for Mary supported her in every way she could, having her for meals at her house in London, inviting her and Raine for weekends at her estate in Cambridgeshire, and even taking Barbara on holiday to the South of France.

But apart from Mary, Barbara was very guarded in her relations now with women. For she knew quite well that after the scandal of a big divorce — and with her present straitened circumstances — she might be snubbed or patronised by some of the hostesses she had known. Typically she had not the least intention of being either.

'I've never admitted to myself that I've been snubbed, and in fact I never had the slightest trouble after my divorce. People didn't ignore me. Rather the reverse.'

For, as she insists, she simply had no wish to go to the sort of parties or grand social gatherings Mayfair wives might have invited — or not invited — Barbara to attend. Cocktail parties had always bored her, and to this day she refuses to attend them — 'an appalling waste of time'. As in the days before her marriage, what she really liked was male company — the more the merrier. Her definition of a perfect party was 'dinner with a man I find attractive and who thinks I'm wonderful'. And as she knew, men were not really interested in the sort of gossip that enthralled their womenfolk. She found she rarely had to dine at home.

The only sign she gave of being just a little less romantic than she used to be came in the answer that she gave to a newspaper questionnaire at the end of 1932 on what she would prefer — true love or a million pounds. Her immediate reply was very much the voice of the Barbara of her youth.

'I would rather have love than a million pounds,' she answered quickly, 'although one perfect love affair sounds rather limiting. Love is life, youth, vitality, and if one loses these, money is hardly any use, however many millions one has.' But then a more worldly-wise Barbara took over as she continued, 'Perhaps on second thoughts if I were offered the choice now, without any further conditions, I would settle for the million, and be content with my own imperfect but very charming present loves.' The truth was that even now, while the crusading side of Barbara was battling for her day-to-day survival, the romantic Barbara, longing to be cosseted, was still as powerful as ever.

In 1977, Barbara managed to arouse the ire of the Women's Liberation Movement when she unequivocally proclaimed that, 'A career girl is a second-rate pseudo-man who looks her worst in trousers and all that a woman really wants is the protection of marriage.' But this was no new conclusion she had hurriedly adopted, for as far back as 1933, when she was a single woman, successfully managing her own career, she was already speaking out against the so-called 'modern woman' of the Thirties.

'I think the modern woman has gone quite mad,' she wrote then in the magazine, *Town Talk*. 'The real woman should be completely feminine, and have no desire to take up a career or flaunt herself in public life. Women should stick to managing their men!'

About the same time she also wrote about the romantic signs a woman values most. Orchids were one of them, and Barbara called them 'the feminine medals of success. As a woman enters a room wearing those absurdly expensive purple blossoms, she knows quite well that they are a sign to every other woman there that she has made a conquest.'

There were also jewels.

It is a man's privilege to decorate the woman that he loves with precious stones, and if there isn't a man to do it, most women will go without. This is the Eastern complex in women – that sense of being possessed, ruled and protected which they pretend that they have killed by emancipation. But on the contrary, women still want to be looked after, loved, and above all, paid for by men.

She really had the best of both worlds now. For Barbara the career girl did as well as any 'modern woman' of the Thirties, while the romantic Barbara never had to buy her own orchids. On the surface she was a sophisticated woman of the world. Her youthful prettiness was changing to mature beauty, her earlier naïvety to an older woman's knowledge of society and men. But underneath she had not really changed. Throughout the many love affairs that followed in this period, she desperately clung to romance and femininity. She longed for marriage and more children, especially a son.

She was still rather like her earliest heroines, still looking for that handsome, slightly cynical dark lover who would sweep her off her feet and worship her. But she insists: 'I never, never chased a man, however much I liked the look of him. If the telephone didn't ring for me, too bad! Nothing on earth would have made me ring him.'

She also went on acting rather like a virgin. 'I believed a man who was in love with me had to teach me everything – and when I was in love it was so new, exciting and different he filled the whole world and I could not remember there had ever been anyone else.'

And though she fell slightly in love repeatedly, and had now added to that score of forty-nine proposals, she never seemed to find her ideal husband. Michael Arlen made a determined pass at her, but she found the author of *The Green Hat* 'perfectly revolting', and rebuffed him out of hand. The heir to an Earldom had proposed to her for years and went on hoping, but although he was intelligent he was also rather pompous, untidy and unsmart.

He would inherit one of the finest houses in England which would have made Polly very happy, but Barbara said she 'could not marry a house'. He however also became one of her life-long friends and though she often stayed in the house which could have been hers, she had no regrets.

No one really took Glen Kidston's place – until she went to the South of France with the Cunningham-Reids and met the man who should have made her happy. The situation might have been described by Elinor Glyn herself – the luxury hotel, a speed boat, evenings at the casino, and Barbara dancing with a fair-haired young Englishman who was staying with mutual friends in a famous villa after the breakup of his first unhappy marriage.

He was widely travelled, and extremely charming. His father was a Marquis, who held high office overseas. Like Barbara he was lonely, seeking an idealised, perfect love. She has described that first day they met and how, 'We looked into each other's eyes and knew we were meant for each other since the beginning of time.'

For Barbara this was her first truly carefree holiday since long before the breakup of her marriage, and she believed that finally the struggle and the bitterness of life were over. Not merely was he charming, attentive and very much in love, he was also strong and intelligent enough to make her happily accept that secondary role she really longed for with a man. Back in London they continued to see one another every day and they planned their marriage the moment they were both free from the six months' wait which in those days was compulsory after the final decree.

'Everything,' she wrote, 'should have been perfect.'

But just when it seemed that happiness was finally within her grasp, 'fate, that strange, mysterious power against which there is no appeal, decreed otherwise'. Some time before in India the man she loved, who was fair-skinned, had developed eczema, from riding with his Regiment in the excessive heat. He had been cured by the newly fashionable treatment of radium. At the time the doctors failed to realise the genetic dangers of radiation, but when he met Barbara he already knew the truth, and he confessed to her that the radium had made him incapable of having children. As his parents' only child, he would inherit his father's title, but it would die with him.

For Barbara this was the cruellest of blows. True she already had a daughter she loved dearly, but she was desperate to have more children, especially sons to carry on the family that meant so much to her. She could have ignored the problem and continued with the marriage, but she knew herself well enough by now to realise how fatal such a course would be.

After one failed marriage she knew how insidiously any frustration connected with the physical side of marriage could destroy love. She felt incapable of risking such unhappiness a second time. Better to part now with the memory of the brief rapture they had known together. It took courage, but Barbara knew it was the only way, and twenty years later she still remembered the misery of that irrevocable parting. She wrote a poem about it which she entitled, 'So Long a Time'.

> Is it twenty years since you said good-bye?
> I remember your roses made me cry.
> And your letter which said so little and yet
> I knew it was something I'd never forget.
>
> Twenty years and I can still hear
> That note in your voice when our lips were near,
> The feel of your arms, your mouth, your hands
> Encompass me still like unbreakable bands.
>
> I laugh, seem busy and people say,
> 'It's wonderful how you are always gay.'
> But when I think of you I know
> Those twenty years have been slow . . . slow . . . slow.

Because she was lonely and unhappy she was intrigued by an ardent tempestuous wooing which was an echo of the dramatics of the Twenties. Tall, dark and slightly cynical, after a disastrous marriage to a famous politicians' daughter, this suitor was the only son of a tycoon reputed to be the richest man in the world. He was infatuated with Barbara but again there was a flaw – he drank. One evening when he had behaved badly in public she said goodbye and told him she had no wish to see him again.

She was awoken the next morning when he burst into her bedroom, having bribed her maid to let him in. He flung himself on his knees beside her, begging forgiveness and as a peace offering proffered her a diamond bracelet he had waited outside Cartiers to buy as the shop opened. But as Ethel M. Dell had always said, 'Money can't buy love!'

CHAPTER SIX

'My Other Self'

Barbara has long been obsessed by what she calls, 'the world behind the world' – the spiritual dimension to which everyone belongs but which is beyond our immediate perception. Unlike Polly, who would soon become a Roman Catholic and lived a life of dedicated Christian piety, Barbara is not conventionally religious. As she puts it, she isn't 'Churchy', for she mistrusts the way that organised religions seem to lose their message in their ritual, whilst with Christianity she finds the doctrines of guilt and sin abhorrent. 'I simply refuse to be told that I am a miserable sinner,' she exclaims. 'I'm not.'

Instead she believes in what she calls 'the power-house' of the spirit, the mystical dimension of eternity to which human beings yearn and which she believes to be the source of the all-important 'Life Force' animating every one of us. As she has written, 'We are vital, magnetic, wonderful, transcending, and through our beautiful bodies we can give out the life rays and control the power which is greater than the universe, and reach divinity through our consciousness.'

Life for her has been a conscious effort to develop these resources in herself. She believes firmly in the power of prayer, as a way of contacting her 'power-house'. She prays before she makes a decision or a speech, and is convinced that she draws her strength and her vitality to produce her books from this all-important spiritual source. She has also long believed that the true purpose of existence is for each individual to develop just this sort of spiritual strength – what she has called a 'big' personality – by overcoming the disasters and the disappointments of this mortal life.

Certainly she did this during the heartache and the struggle to survive after the breakup of her marriage. Even her decision to give up the man she fell in love with in the South of France strengthened her and finally became a sort of triumph, simply because she knew that she was right.

One of the key ideas she had absorbed from Ethel M. Dell had been the spiritual force of passionate love. 'Love,' as Barbara wrote, 'is the supreme ingredient of the Life Force. Everything "big" derives from love.' And therefore she consoled herself with the thought that, 'It is impossible to "love and lose". Love when we give or take it becomes part of us. We absorb it into ourselves. Once absorbed, we can never lose it. Therefore don't moan when a lover leaves you. Never regret, and never look back at the past except with gratitude.'

It was easy to say this, but Barbara would have been less than human had she not felt the misery that every woman knows at the end of an affair. She was fortunate to find an unexpected source of strength and resolution, at this moment when she needed it, in the elder of her two brothers, Ronald.

She had always been extremely close to him – more so, than to Tony, the carefree youngest child who was eleven years her junior. Tony despite all Polly's efforts to instil in him ambition and a dedicated sense of purpose, had managed to remain rather like his father as a young man – an easy-going, handsome charmer who got on well with everybody. Like his brother he had gone to Charterhouse, and he already saw his future in the regular Army. But although he would enjoy the Army, and keep Polly happy by assuring her that he would end up a Field Marshal, Barbara insists that what he really liked was 'the company of his friends, a good cigar and a pretty girl'.

Ronald was very different. He had been deeply influenced by his mother, by her religion and her insistence that he must carry on his father's work after his death in France. His boyish dreams of being a politician – just as Bertie would have been – had never left him.

He was an idealist: whilst at Charterhouse he had once supported Socialism in a school debate, and according to a report in the *Carthusian*,

Cartland tried to shatter our complacency by telling us that we were not fit for the manure heap. He said that we were soaked in a rotten tradition, the result of which was the late war. . . . We were stagnating, were liars and uneducated. He concluded by pointing out . . . that 'Socialism was not Communism'.

Ronald was not a Socialist himself. When his political beliefs had formed, he found himself a Conservative, like his father; but he retained much of that youthful, non-conformist zeal he showed in the school debate. He still felt the need to speak out against complacency, and believed passionately in combining practical politics with Christian principles. Like Barbara he had a desperate desire to achieve. When he had told her he intended to be Prime Minister, he meant it.

But after leaving school his hopes had seemed to falter. There had been no money for University, and a bad accident – he had nearly lost a leg in a shooting mishap – blighted his chances of a lucrative business career. Polly had nursed him back to health, and in 1927, at the age of twenty-one he began work, at £3 a week, as a research assistant at the Conservative Central Office in Westminster. His political career had started.

Since then he had devoted himself to politics and politicians with true Cartland single-mindedness, getting to know the leading figures of the day, briefing his party members on official policy, and working long hours both at Central Office and behind the scenes in the House of Commons. He had no money except what he earned and at one time Polly had had to settle up his debts rather as she had done with Bertie. When Barbara lived in Culross Street, he often had his one good meal of the week when he came to dine with her. But it was not until the time of the divorce that she really got to know him.

For as well as persuading Patrick Hastings to take on her case, he was the staunchest of supporters for his sister. Instinctively he seemed to understand what she was going through. He knew her well enough to recognise the signs of wretchedness behind the brave front she was putting on, and it was his suggestion that they should go off together for a short holiday in France not long before the case came up in Court. They chose the little spa of Brides-les-Bains in the mountains of the French Savoie, and according to Barbara,

It was the first of our wonderful holidays together when I discovered a happiness I had ever known before, that of perfect companionship. He loved walking and we would walk six or seven miles every afternoon. . . . We talked of politics, of religion; we formulated our philosophy of living and took courage from our faith in ourselves and in each other.

It was a crucial discovery for them both, and it was partly Ronald's influence that accounts for the calmness she displayed in Court, for budding professional politician that he was, he carefully rehearsed her for her ordeal by asking her every tricky question he could think of, so that she could practise her replies.

From this time on, Barbara and Ronald were very close. In some ways it was a strange relationship, for both of them continued with their separate lives, their separate love affairs, and both were furiously busy with their work. But none of this prevented them from drawing steadily closer until they might have been a pair of twins. Soon they had no secrets from each other. Ronald began correcting Barbara's novels as she wrote them, and they telephoned each other twice a day.

By now Polly had sold her flat in London and had returned to her beloved Worcestershire – to a small, black-and-white, sixteenth-century, half-timbered house called Littlewood House at Poolbrook, a pretty village close to Malvern. Ronald and Barbara spent their weekends here. There was a pool where

Ronald loved to swim, an orchard where they sat beneath the apple-trees, and both of them would walk for miles across the Malvern Hills.

It was now that Barbara really turned to religion, and began to think out her beliefs. Polly had brought her up as a conventional Christian. She prayed, she went to Church, and much of her earliest morality came for her strict beliefs. But as she also readily admits, she was 'very superstitious'. As a child she had believed firmly in the other world of ghosts and fairies. Nailsea Court, where she had lessons for three years, she says was haunted, and she had found herself particularly receptive to any sort of pyschic happening.

Even before the divorce she had become fascinated by mystical religion, and was reading everything she could 'on Tibet, on Yoga and reincarnation.' Soon she was reporting that, 'I am practising Yoga breathing, and now I can often hear music when I listen and at night I have dreams which are vivid with colour and leave me with an intense feeling of happiness'.

But it was Ronald who really enabled her to sort out her ideas. For he had already been reading systematically. He placed more emphasis than Barbara on the importance of the Church, but he was also absorbed by the study of esoteric cults, of theosophy and the religions of the East.

According to Barbara, 'Ronald taught me everything I know about spiritual things' – the power of prayer, the nature of the universe, and the importance of love. One of the first books he gave her was Ouspensky's *New Model for the Universe* with its invigorating message that, 'All religion, all myths, all beliefs, all prophecies, heroic legends of all people and all countries, are based on the recognition of the existence sometime and somewhere of a knowledge far superior to the knowledge we possess.'

It was an idea which inspired them both, and much of their time was spent in deep discussion of its implications. It was from Ronald that she got the idea of the 'spiritual power-station' and of the everyday world as what he called a 'classroom' in which every individual had the chance to learn the lessons of his spiritual being. They argued over how they both should learn these lessons. Barbara was in favour of withdrawal from the world, but Ronald taught her that one had a duty to remain within the world and try to alter it through love.

They both thought the act of sex alone was 'very unimportant', so was death, since both of them were convinced of the truth of reincarnation, and the final passing of the spirit to the 'Fourth Dimension'. This was to be a source of strength to both of them – and particularly to Barbara – during the years to come.

By now they were virtually inseparable. 'Ronald was like my other self. We thought alike, wanted identical things, and could almost have been one person.'

They were both certain they had been together in other lives. Perhaps as brother and sister, or father and daughter, even in changed sexes. That was immaterial beside the fact that they were indivisible.

Their separate love affairs continued, but by now they seemed increasingly irrelevant. For Barbara's great romantic quest was really over. She had found the man she needed, her man of destiny, the superior being who alone could make her happy in the shadow of his success. The only irony was that it had to be her brother.

'Every man I met,' says Barbara, 'seemed so inferior to Ronald now. I stimulated his mind and he mine. In fact we were essential to each other and we were both perfectly happy when we were together. He had a vitality which made the tempo rise and when we were together, it was magnetic.'

In August 1933 they went off on holiday again. For Barbara and Ronald it was one of the crucial moments of their lives.

Ronald had recently grown friendly with the novelist Rom Landau, and largely on his suggestion they decided to visit Austria.

Neither had been there before, but from the moment that they stepped aboard the Arlberg-Orient Express, it was like a period romance. They woke to a clear blue sky and the snowy peaks of the Austrian Alps. They caught their first glimpse of the Danube from the carriage windows, and when they reached Vienna the capital of love and music cast its inevitable spell over them both.

The Hotel Meissl und Schadn was like some caravanserai of eighteenth-century romance. Our rooms were enormous, they must have been used by the Arch-duke himself we told each other. In one corner of my bedroom was a huge, blue-tiled stove for the cold weather, the walls were hung with icons and the sheets were buttoned over the blankets to make a kind of thin counterpane which cannot be tucked in. The rooms were filled with the fragrance of fresh carnations which Ronald had ordered for me as a surprise.

They both enjoyed Vienna for its opera and its cafés and its carefree-seeming people. But for both of them the most memorable moment came in the great Cathedral, the Stephans-Dom. Barbara felt at once, 'the most moving atmosphere of any place I have ever visited'.

They felt that here in the Cathedral they were close to the spirit of the real Vienna with its sense of everlasting hope despite the war and famine which had plagued the city. And it was while they watched the people come to pray in the candlelight before the miraculous picture of the Immaculate Conception, that Barbara clearly saw the ghostly figure of a Cardinal.

He was outlined against the dark stone of the Cathedral so clearly as to show his features and the expression on his face. It was deeply lined with suffering, but he had an expression of serenity and compassion, of faith transcending all the cruelties, the bestialities, and the stupidities of mankind. He remained with me for a long while.

From Vienna Barbara and Ronald moved on to the little village of Seeboden on the shores of a pretty lake in Carinthia. As they spoke barely any German, they caused much puzzlement to the villagers, especially when they insisted on renting separate rooms in a little chalet by the lake.

They bathed in the lake, ate venison and wild strawberries, listened to the German band that played in the village café, and every afternoon climbed in the surrounding mountains. It was during one of these expeditions that they saw a distant castle. They had been caught in a sudden downpour and the castle on the far side of a lake appeared enchanted, 'as if the fairy palaces one dreamt of in the nursery had come to life'. A flag was flying from one of its many turrets.

Barbara was instantly agog to visit it and see inside, but they were drenched and Ronald promised they would visit it the following afternoon. They tried, and failed to find it, and continued with their search for several days. Then finally they found the lake again, but when they crossed to see the castle, all they could find were ruins – broken walls, an ivy-covered tower, the remains of an enormous courtyard.

It was a haunting little episode that troubled Barbara even when they left for England a few days later. Inevitably she wondered if it could be a portent of disaster. A few days later Ronald told her that a Nazi rising had just broken out in the streets of beautiful Vienna, with savage fighting in the very streets where they had been sitting just a few weeks earlier.

Barbara's career was now beginning to improve, for in addition to her publicity work, she was increasingly successful as a journalist. Soon after her divorce, Comyns Beaumont had made her social Editress of the *National Graphic* magazine, and since then she had established a unique position for herself as what she calls 'a lone wolf working journalist'.

She still took on the occasional publicity campaign that interested her. For example, at the end of 1933 she was drumming up interest in the Duke of Atholl's Fund, an attempt by its distinguished sponsor to provide a London-based alternative to the Irish Sweep Stake in the hope of benefiting English charities.

But her real flair was journalism and in 1933 she landed the journalistic scoop of the year when she broke the story of the notorious 'prisoner in the Tower'. Through a close friend she had picked up the sensational news that a British Army officer, Lieutenant Norman Baillie-Stewart, was being held prisoner in the Tower of London on suspicion of selling secrets to the Germans. None of the regular Fleet Street newshawks had got wind of it, and the story made front page headlines in the *Express*. It also confirmed Barbara's growing reputation as one of the best informed freelance journalists in London and soon she had more work than even she could cope with.

Most of it she did anonymously, for it suited her to work behind the scenes and she had seen enough of journalism to know how journalists were treated – and how remorselessly they were 'got at' – when their names were known. For a while she was the well-informed 'Miss Tudor' in the *Daily Mail*. As 'Miss Hamilton' she invented a novel gossip-column which she called 'Caviare' in the weekly *Bystander* magazine. 'Miss Scott' wrote for three years the weekly social 'Panorama' in the *Tatler*, and her most prestigious piece of all was the weekly social article in the Sunday *Observer*. Her identity remained a closely-guarded secret, and even the formidable Lady Astor failed to persuade the proprietor of the *Observer*, Waldorf Astor, to tell her who the mysterious journalist was.

Barbara's anonymity as a journalist had another great advantage. It enabled her to live her private life and to enjoy herself, and it was now that her serenity returned. The nightmare that had followed the divorce had vanished, and rather to her surprise she found that she was happy.

This was primarily due to Ronald, but there were other causes too. One was her family. All her life she has always been an intensely 'family' person, only finding true security and happiness within her home with those she loves. Divorce had temporarily robbed her of this refuge, but the maisonette in Half Moon Street had now become a proper home, and Raine had changed from a baby into an enchanting five-year-old. Although Barbara had always been very much the 'working mother' she had been determined to bring up Raine just as Polly had done with her, and the absence of a father in the house had brought them even closer than they might have been.

Rather like Polly too, Barbara already had ambitions for her daughter. Raine was extremely pretty – and obviously intelligent – and from the start Barbara brought her up to make the most of her potential. Early in 1933 there was a revealing glimpse of her among a round-up of 'Society Children' published in *Vogue* magazine.

Raine McCorquodale sits in the nursery window on her rocking-horse: you have a fine view of Curzon Street from Raine's windows and the little daughter of 'Barbara Cartland' is a perfect hostess for the after-tea visitor. Mrs McCorquodale believes in making her small blonde daughter a good mixer straight away, so that the shyness and weariness of parties may not worry her later. So Raine has achieved a pretty dignity of manners which should stand her in good stead later.

Raine was already an extraordinarily composed and self-reliant five-year-old, as the article makes clear.

Her mantelpiece is covered with invitation cards and her engagement diary must be almost as full as mother's. One leaves her sitting down before bedtime to write her letters, her lovely fairness gilded by the candles to make the scene, and appropriately arranged against a friendly, familiar background of toys, firelight – and Nannie.

It was inevitable that Barbara's struggles and her sometimes harsh experience of life should have found their way into the novels she was writing now, and it is interesting to see how her earliest virgin heroines begin to change. As she says, 'During the 1930s I wrote a lot of books around the theme of unhappy marriages, because I had been through all that myself. Inevitably books like mine tend to be autobiographical.'

Cinderella has now become a married woman – even a woman of the world – and the novels of this period offer a fascinating insight into Barbara's views of women in society. One of her early novels of this period, which she called simply, *For What?* chronicles the story of a pretty innocent who makes the mistake of marrying 'an almost painfully silent Scottish laird' before her mind is properly made up over whether or not she really loves him. Too late she discovers that she doesn't, and when pregnant falls fatally in love with another man. The story, unlike almost every other Barbara Cartland novel, ends unhappily.

More intriguing still, with its faithfully reported vignettes of the London society Barbara knew so well, is the most daring of the novels that she ever wrote. She entitled it *Sweet Punishment*, and it tells the story of the spoiled and arrogant society beauty, Lady Diana Stanlier.

Her beauty, which caused envy and admiration in the hearts of all women, was portrayed in most photographers' windows, hung on the walls of the Academy, and featured in every picture paper. If there was a pageant, here was the Queen of beauty. If there was a crusade, a charitable appeal, or a national protestation, Diana headed the list; if there was a race to be won, a flight to be made, or an experiment to be proved on road, on sea or in the air, Diana was invariably the first to attempt, the first to achieve. And she was rich, she was beautiful and she was witty.

In addition to all this, 'Diana lived on love, and lived dangerously, but that was the only life which she desired, the only entertainment which really amused her'.

She was the sort of woman Barbara had frequently observed at first-hand in the past, and the action starts when Diana Stanlier attempts to trifle with the affections of a genuine red-blooded Cartland hero. Sun-tannned, six-foot three, laird of a Scottish Castle in the Western Isles, and just returned to the old country after untold hardships in East Africa, Ian Carstairs is the sort of lover Barbara herself had often dreamed of as a girl and had hoped to find in Alexander.

His nature had been pent up for so many years. He had repressed and subdued his feelings with all the sternness of Scottish reserve; but, like a volcano, they had errupted into an overwhelming passion and with a force that he could not control. He wanted Diana, and he meant to have her.

Have her he does – after the unspeakable Diana sneeringly rejects his manly declaration of undying love. She wants to make a fool of him, but she should have known better. Indeed she could have taken warning from her namesake, Lady Diana Conway, the heroine of E.M. Hull's romance, *The Sheik*. She too had tried to trifle with the feelings of a silent handsome hero, and Ian Carstairs acts with all the brisk decision of his dusky counterpart.

The Mayfair vamp is kidnapped in his aeroplane, flown to his hereditary stronghold in the Western Isles, and guarded by the Carstairs family retainers.

What does he intend to do with her, she asks somewhat shakily, after a silent meal with her captor in the great hall of the thirteenth-century Castle?

'Wouldn't you treat a murderer as a murderer?' he replied.
Diana hesitated. 'Yes, I suppose so.'
'And a woman who behaves like a harlot as a harlot?'
Diana put down her cup a little hastily and rose to her feet. . . . She was desperately afraid.

But there is nothing she can do, and Ian takes her to the ancestral bedroom.

'I want you, Diana' – and his voice was deep with desire. Wildly

Diana sought to escape. She glanced feverishly around the room – but she was imprisoned.

'I despise and detest you,' she said, slowly and feelingly. 'Does that attract you?'

'Immensely,' he answered, smiling. 'A complacent woman is often a bore. . . .'

His arms enclosed her, she fought against him wildly and there was the sound of rending.

Breathless, her hair dishevelled, her shoulder bare through the torn lace, she pushed him from her for a second. Very lovely she was at that moment, her dark eyes wide, distended and blazing with anger.

Ian caught her to him again.

'Fight, my beautiful – fight – it makes me want you more!'. . . .

Her dress ripped and was thrown in a crumpled heap on the floor. The firelight gleamed on the whiteness of her body. . . . She cried out but there was no one to hear her, and, helpless, he carried her triumphantly into the shadows of the great bed.

Diana finally escapes from the island, and returns to London. But in her heart of hearts the once arrogant beauty now knows that she has met her match and is hopelessly in love with her romantic ravisher. Her kidnapping by the decisive Ian Carstairs represents a victory for the very qualities of life which Barbara herself admires – manliness, honesty, romantic passion and ancestral feeling – over the perverted and dishonest world of smart society. Assertive womanhood has been tamed by its rightful master, the dominating male. And honest passion has finally proved more powerful than what Barbara calls 'this dish of indecency, perverted sex and dirt' in the frenetic, money-grubbing, sex-obsessed world of fashionable London in the early Thirties.

So a very changed Diana finally returns to the isle of her captivity and wins the man she needs – in marriage.

CHAPTER SEVEN

'Men Matter Most'

For a woman who has achieved wealth, fame and success by her own unaided efforts, Barbara has a somewhat unexpected philosophy on the subject of a woman's ideal role in life.

In history her favourite heroines are not the great achievers like Joan of Arc or Elizabeth I. She much prefers such purely feminine women as Elizabeth of Austria and Napoleon's wife, Josephine, or better still, the lovely Diane de Poitiers, who even in old age remained the influential and adored mistress of the King of France, Henri II.

Her secret dream has always been to change the world by influencing the man she loves, and she insists that she would have willingly exchanged all her personal success in life for such a role.

As early as the beginning of 1936 she was writing in an article in *Pearson's Weekly*, in answer to the question, 'What matters most to women?',

Men matter most! . . .
The trouble with most women today is that they will not realise that women can only succeed when they are the inspiration or the shadow *behind* men: that men become great through them. That is the secret of women's power.'

It was the cruellest twist of Barbara's life, that the one man she could successfully have done this with, turned out to be her brother, Ronald.

Even so she did in fact act as a spur and inspiration to him. No sooner were they back in England in the autumn of 1933 after their holiday in Austria than she became responsible for one of the key decisions of his life. Barbara vividly recalls the moment still. It was a late Tuesday afternoon in the middle of October, and Ronald had walked across the Park from his office in Westminster to have a late tea with Barbara at her flat. Something had obviously excited him.

'What do you think? I've just heard that Major Beaumont-Thomas isn't seeking re-election at King's Norton. It's the seat I've always wanted.'

'You must put your name forward then,' Barbara said.

'As official party candidate for the seat? You must be mad.'

'Not at all. It's obviously meant for you. I'm as certain of it as I am of anything in the world.'

Ronald remained unconvinced. At twenty-six he was young – and totally inexperienced – for a career in Parliament. More serious still, he had no money of his own, and knew quite well that a Conservative candidate would need a minimum of £1,000 for electoral expenses. He said that he would never dream of standing as a party hack, paid for and tied hand and foot by Central Office. Not that there seemed much chance of this occurring, for Ronald also knew that there would be keen competition for the Conservative nomination to an important Birmingham constituency like King's Norton.

But Barbara was adamant that Ronald should apply. Money was neither here nor there. A thousand pounds might seem an enormous sum to both of them, but they would find it somehow, if only they had faith in one another. That faith had never let them down in the past – it wouldn't now. Barbara had never felt so certain about anything before. Whatever happened, Ronald's name must go forward for the seat. He finally agreed.

Apart from her intuitive belief that this was right for Ronald, Barbara had another reason for encouraging him. King's Norton had a very special meaning for the Cartlands. For on the edge of the constituency, an oasis from the past among the encroaching factories of industrial Birmingham, stood the house and small untouched estate of The Priory, with the Cartland crest above the door.

Four generations of the family had lived here. It had survived the ruin of their grandfather, the financier James Cartland; and his brother, their eccentric great-uncle Howard was still there. Cartland Road ran along the constituency boundary, and there were Cartlands buried in King's Norton Church.

Typically, once the decision had been made, Barbara lost no time in finding influential backers for her brother. That weekend she was off to Scotland for a smart house-party and among the guests was the forceful figure of a Conservative statesman. He made a dead set at Barbara and as their bedrooms were close together in an isolated part of the Castle suggested it was an 'unique opportunity'. Barbara refused him very firmly but felt justified in asking his advice for Ronald. His words were very much in character. Ronald should do exactly what he felt he had to. 'Never let lack of money stand in the way of an opportunity,' he grandiloquently declared.

Barbara answered that this was all very well, but that her brother was all but penniless. The statesman replied that he would see him and if he liked him would support him personally. He wrote Barbara some passionate poems and was as good as his word. He liked Ronald from the moment that they met and as a Birmingham MP himself, sent off an influential private letter of recommendation to the selectors of King's Norton.

Barbara soon helped whip up other supporters – including the family's standby, Sir Bolton Eyres Monsell, who was now First Lord of the Admiralty, David Margesson, the Conservative Chief Whip, and an important MP, the blustering Sir Patrick Hannon. Ronald's prospects were already looking up, and the selectors recommended him over the heads of more than twenty other candidates.

His great test came at the end of November when the Executive Committee of the local party were making their decision. It was

Ronald's duty to address them, and everything depended on his speech. This time Barbara rehearsed him through it all beforehand and practised every sentence with him – just as he had done with her at the time of the divorce. Barbara and Polly were both in the hall to hear him make his solemn declaration, pledging himself, if chosen, to work ceaselessly for international peace, for the Empire and for the interests of the voters of King's Norton. But Ronald also warned his listeners that, if they chose him for their candidate, they would not find him a political weather-vane. He had his principles, and he would always act on them.

Ronald possessed unusual power when he spoke in public, and the adoption meeting proved to be a triumph. He was voted for unanimously, and at twenty-six was suddenly prospective candidate for the traditional constituency of the Cartlands.

This marked the beginning of a frantic period of work for Barbara, for Ronald needed all the help that he could muster if he was ever going to win King's Norton at the next election. There was already a powerful Labour opponent in the person of G. R. Mitchison, the economist husband of the well-known novelist, Naomi Mitchison. Mitchison was popular, particularly with the local car-workers who made up an important section of the vote. He had already had several years to nurse the constituency, and his political machine was far ahead of the Conservatives'. Ronald was also handicapped by his youth, his apparent inexperience, and the fact that he was virtually unknown. Hardly surprisingly, Mitchison was odds-on favourite for the seat. It would be an uphill battle to get Ronald to Westminster.

But Ronald had a secret weapon of his own – the energy and the ambition of the Cartlands. The family had never been more powerful and more united than they were now. Luckily they had a useful ally, and something of a base already at The Priory, for their great-uncle Major Howard Cartland with his dog-cart and his jaunty manner was a well-loved character in the neighbourhood and something of an eccentric local squire. Polly was there to offer her support among the older Party faithfuls — she organised splendid weekend teas for motor-coach loads of Conservative ladies at Littlewood House — and barely a weekend went by without Barbara joining Ronald in the humdrum business of ward meetings, canvassing, street-corner meetings and addressing envelopes.

Occasionally that well-known lady novelist, Miss Mitchison, would clash with that other well-known lady novelist, Miss Cartland. And throughout these early meetings, Ronald never wavered in the unusual moral tone that he adopted. Politically he was the most open-minded of Conservatives and he was already making it quite clear that, if he got to Parliament, he would never be simple lobby-fodder for his Party. On the other hand, he was already preaching the sort of Christian message that Barbara could understand, but which was most unusual among candidates of any party.

Our philosophy, as Unionists [he stated in an early speech] rests on the belief that a man's life in this world rests on a preparation for the next; that the soul of man is more important than his body, and that as far as is possible in the state of society in which he lives, a man should be allowed to work out his destiny in his own way. . . .

We live in the world as it is; we strive to better it, but we realise that the Kingdom of God is above and it is man's soul that will attain to it — not man's body. No Government can change men's souls.

Once he got going, Ronald proved something of a spell-binder with an audience, and his visionary message started to attract support. But money still remained an over-riding problem. It was all very well to say that lack of it should never stand between a man and his opportunities, but there were times when the young Conservative candidate for King's Norton could barely find the money for a ticket to his constituency. He lived on sandwiches and buns and early in 1935 was so depressed by his poverty that he wrote to Polly saying that he was seriously thinking of giving up and retiring to a monastery. 'B. is optimistic, ' he wrote, 'but alas I'm not.' It was largely Barbara's optimism now that kept him going, and she supported him financially as well. To do this she was having to increase her journalistic work, and often wrote 10,000 words of her current novel as a daily stint. (By now she had luckily adopted Godfrey Winn's advice, and was dictating every book, otherwise she never would have managed.) Thanks to her efforts, during 1935, she was able to pay £150 into Ronald's electoral fund, and guarantee his overdraft for an additional £350. And that August, seeing how worn out and depressed he had become, and with an election forecast for the autumn, she insisted on taking him on holiday again.

Raine was dispatched to stay in Worcestershire with Polly – the two of them were already devoted to each other – and Barbara and Ronald both decided that after the success of the previous year in Austria, it was time that they saw Germany. It turned out rather differently from what they hoped, and proved a formative experience – particularly for Ronald.

Even the first part of the holiday – aboard the German luxury liner, *Bremen*, from Southampton to Bremerhaven – was something of an ordeal, with filthy cabins, until Barbara made a scene. They travelled to Berlin by rail – and found the churches closed. There were official Nazi Party ordinances against women's makeup, so that Barbara was uncomfortably stared at in the streets. Even the little village in Bavaria where they spent their holiday was disturbing. There were anti-Jewish posters in the streets, unsmiling members of the Hitler Youth tramping through the countryside, and heavily armed German Panzer troops massing near the Austrian frontier. Ronald was particularly suspicious when he saw that German engineers were busily enlarging the old one-track railway that led below the Zugspitz into Austria.

It was hard not to be impressed by the beauty of Bavaria, but Barbara and Ronald were agreed on one thing when they returned to England – their deep dislike of Nazi Germany, and an uneasy feeling that none of the Germans would be satisfied until they were at war with Britain. This was an uncomfortable belief for a young Conservative to hold in 1935, when so many of the party leaders were convinced that Germany was our natural ally. But from now on a deep conviction of the evil and the threat of Nazism dominated Ronald's thought – and would rule his actions and his loyalties for the remainder of his life.

Thanks largely to the need for money to back Ronald at King's Norton, 1935 proved one of the most productive years for Barbara. Apart from a steady, and increasingly lucrative stream of journalism, Barbara also published *First Class, Lady?*, which she has described as an 'unmoral' story about Mayfair mannequins, and her 'most glamorous book since *A Virgin in Mayfair*'. For once Polly disliked it – normally she enthusiastically approved of everything that Barbara wrote – and those guardians of stern morality, the Government of the Irish Free State, banned it. Perhaps because of this, *First Class, Lady?* sold better than any of Barbara's other books to date.

Then, just a few weeks later, Barbara published a completely different sort of book, something that few of the regular readers of her romantic novels would have expected. It was entitled, *Touch the Stars – A Clue to Happiness*, and represented an attempt by Barbara to explain that personal philosophy of life which she and Ronald had worked out during their walks across the Malvern Hills.

Throughout her life, Barbara has always had an impulse to speak out for causes she believes in. She traces this back to Polly who originally instilled in all her children the Victorian belief that they should somehow change society for the better and improve the world by their example. Polly had tried to do this by her dedicated work among the poor. Ronald was doing it by trying to bring his spiritual values into politics. Even the light-hearted Tony in his way was following the course of duty: early in 1935 as a subaltern in the Lincolnshire Regiment, he had been sent to Egypt as ADC to the Commander in Chief and was reported to be doing well.

Touch the Stars was Barbara's contribution to the cause of human betterment. As she wrote in the Introduction, 'Many people have asked me in the last year,' "Why are you so happy?" . . . and I have written this little book in the hope that some word or thought in it might stimulate them towards a realisation of the vast possibilities of attainable happiness in this world.'

She goes on to say that the theories she puts forward in the book are her own personal rules which she has worked out for herself, and which 'have helped me through a difficult period of my life'. Because of this, *Touch the Stars* is not only Barbara's private testament – but also an intriguing portrait of its author.

Running through the book is a great deal of Barbara's original bounciness and optimism, as she picks on 'those unfortunates who are drifting aimlessly through life without a guide or are without ambition to succeed'.

'You have got to develop yourself, to improve and grow "big",' she tells them firmly. And how does one do this? 'By experience. Depth of character, a "big" personality comes because one has a real knowledge of life. . . . You yourself have to get down to life, to live it, and only in that experience are you likely to gain understanding, and from that to enlarge your personality and your character.'

Courage is vital in the fight for self-improvement, for as Barbara insists, 'Fear is the most to be loathed, the most degrading of all the emotions of the human mind. It is the enemy of all progress.'

Enemies are unimportant. 'No really intelligent and "big" person bothers about enemies, for this reason: only that which is of use to your development is worth your time, attention and concentration.'

Prayer has its uses, but her views on prayer are not the conventional Christian ones. 'Each time you feel thrilled, ecstatic, splendidly alive, you are linking yourself with the Life Force. And a really honest joy, because you are happy to be alive, and the world is beautiful, is much more elevating to you than prolonged, maybe grumbling prayers upon your knees.'

And finally there is the all-transforming power of romantic love.

Remember that you are not a miserable sinner; you are a fine person of great capabilities, with the possibility of being a 'big' personality. Nor were you born in original sin; the sex instinct is one of the most beautiful things in the world. It is sent to inspire us, and to help us to understand Nature and the workings of the Divine. It is the nearest approach we get to the beauty, the intensity and the power of Life.

Above all, be ambitious. 'Aim high, even the stars are not high enough. And aim for a prize that can never be rewarded in full.'

Ronald was certainly following Barbara's advice, and at the beginning of November when the Election duly started, few of the old political hands in Birmingham gave much for his chances – particularly when he pointedly refused to invite any of the big names in the Party to come and speak for him. Mitchison was bringing down leading Labour politicians like George Lansbury and Sir Stafford Cripps to liven up his meetings, but Ronald wanted to preserve his reputation for total independence. Instead he was relying on a handful of devoted constituency workers, and the immediate support Polly and Barbara could give him.

It turned out to be a furious two weeks of frantic canvassing, with Ronald addressing six or seven meetings in an evening, and Barbara loyally 'holding the fort' till he arrived. Polly of course was there to organise the faithful in the committee rooms, and Major Cartland had guaranteed £500 of his nephew's electoral expenses. Polling Day, 14 November, was a depressing, rainy Birmingham day, and this too was generally thought bad news for Ronald. 'Labour goes to the poll in the rain, but our side can't be bothered,' his agent told him. But the Cartland contingent simply redoubled its efforts, to make sure every supporter that they had turned out, rain or no. They hardly saw each other all that day, and it was nearly midnight when they assembled at the Town Hall for the conclusion of the count and the declaration of the winner.

The Mitchisons and their supporters were in high spirits, for they knew their turn-out had been good, and were taking victory for granted now. The count went on. The tension mounted. And then at one am the Returning Officer rose to announce the result.

The fight was over and, against the heaviest of odds, Ronald was the winner – with a powerful majority of 5,875. Less than two weeks later, Ronald – wearing his father's cuff-links as he had promised Polly that he would – duly took his seat in the House of Commons as Member for King's Norton.

He had succeeded – and so had Barbara, who was in the place where she had always longed to be, in the shadow of the man she loved.

CHAPTER EIGHT

Married Again

Despite the disillusion of Barbara's first unhappy marriage she still — and always has — emphatically believed in marriage as an institution. Not for her the cynical and practical explanation for the popularity of marriage given by Bernard Shaw: 'Because it combines the maximum of temptation with the maximum of opportunity'.

For Barbara, as a true romantic, marriage is nothing less than 'the highest and the most spiritualised form of union that mankind is privileged to enjoy on this planet'. The fact that she had failed to find it so herself was, she admitted, her own fault and 'not the fault of marriage'. With the beginning of the New Year in 1936, it was inevitable that, despite her personal success and her happiness with Ronald, she should have turned her thoughts to marriage once again.

As she realised, Ronald's election to the House of Commons marked a new chapter in their relationship. Barbara had done more than anyone to get him there and launch him on his great career. And now that he was launched, he would inevitably become increasingly bound up with politics, and the fresh loyalties and interests of an ambitious young MP.

But Ronald's success had brought the two of them even closer — if that was possible. Early that summer Barbara helped him organise a massive Chamberlain Centenary Rally at the Albert Hall, and a few weeks later they were off on holiday together once again, this time to France, staying at the tiny village of Begmeil on the coast of Brittany. Here there were none of the distractions which had upset them so in Nazi Germany. Their hotel was set among sand dunes, they could walk for miles along the unspoilt beaches, and had an idyllic holiday, reading, swimming, enjoying the delicious local food – and of course talking non-stop, as they always did when on their own together.

But Barbara was practical enough to know that her relationship with Ronald could not go on for ever as a substitute for marriage. It was all very well to see herself as her brother's twin, and their mental togetherness formed a vital part of both their lives. But she still longed for the closeness of a family of her own. Part of her still wanted to be 'cosseted and worshipped', and the attention of her many male admirers was not the answer. Above all she wanted more children now, preferably boys, and she felt that seven-year-old Raine needed a settled home with other children and a man about the house.

At the same time she understood the difficulties, and knew that any man she married now would have to be rather special. There could be no question of jealousy between him and Ronald, for she had no intention of losing her brother. Nor of course must any husband suffer from those unsuspected weaknesses and failings which had destroyed her life with Alexander. He must be somebody she respected, and who could give her the romantic and the physical love she needed – a strong man, and above all somebody who understood her own romantic, complex, driving nature.

Certainly she had not the least intention now of being swept off her feet by some dangerous, dark-haired, slightly cynical approximation to one of the heroes of her books. She had tried that once with disastrous results. However much her virgin heroines might practice love at first sight, Barbara herself was now intent on being very careful, for she knew too well the dangers, both of instant physical attraction and of sudden romantic love: 'When the stimulation of a flirtation convinces two young people that all is well with their glands, they translate what is little more than ephemeral animal passion into love.'

The answer, she now realised, lay in deeper love, and deeper self-awareness.

In all forms of art, perfection or near-perfection comes after experience and experiment. No masterpiece of music, painting or literature is the first effort of genius. . . . And it is the same with marriage. The only way to avoid matrimonial disaster is to have a deep, ever-increasing knowledge – of LOVE.

She had given herself the time she needed for this sort of knowledge. She was thirty-five and had had more opportunity than most to pick and choose a husband from the innumerable admirers she had attracted during her four successful years of freedom. Some had been very rich. Some had had titles. Some had been dashing, youthful, and flatteringly in love with her. But there was only one man that she knew for certain would be right, and shortly after she returned with Ronald from their holiday in Brittany, she finally accepted him.

It is fascinating that one of the themes throughout her earliest romantic novels concerns the way the heroine is torn between the first romantic love she feels for her husband, and the love she later comes to feel for his brother or his cousin. It is a theme that occurs in *Jigsaw*, the very first novel that she wrote, with the heroine drawn from the humdrum Duke that she married towards his far more dashing brother. It crops up still more forcefully in the depiction of her own unhappy marriage in *If the Tree is Saved*, where the heroine turns from her drunken husband to his strong silent cousin. And in real life Barbara did the same. The man she chose was Alexander's cousin and at one time his closest friend, Hugh McCorquodale.

It was a touching story, for the first time Hugh saw Barbara had in fact been at his cousin's wedding. He met her in the vestry afterwards and always said that there and then he fell in love with her. He had loved her ever since. It was because of her that he had never married, and instead had made a point of being always there to wait for her. Ronald liked him – which was in his favour – but although Barbara felt affection and deep friendship for him almost from the start, her love took several years to grow.

In the meantime she had had various affairs, and was immersed in her relationship with Ronald. But if Hugh felt jealous – as he often did – he rarely showed it, for he knew Barbara well enough to realise that he would never win her through jealousy. Instead she increasingly relied upon him, and whatever happened he was always in the background of her life.

He was a very patient, very gentle man, and in many ways the absolute antithesis of Barbara – quiet where she was flamboyant, tolerant where she was always passionately involved with life, accepting where she was often out to change the world. Everyone who knew him loved him. The family called him Uncle Hugh.

Barbara says that there was hardly a thing that they agreed about. But opposites can form ideal partners, and from taking Hugh for granted, Barbara had gradually found herself in love with him. In certain superficial ways he was rather like his cousin, Alexander: both had been at the same preparatory school; both went to Harrow; both made their money from the family printing business; both were expert fishermen and splendid shots (which meant that, like it or not, Barbara would once again be spending a good part of every holiday on grouse moors or by salmon rivers). Both had served in Scottish Regiments: Alexander in the Argyll and Sutherland Highlanders; Hugh in the Cameron Highlanders. He had won the MC but he had been terribly badly wounded at the Battle of Passchendaele. Barbara was told his expectation of life might be five years. But Hugh was reliable, devoted, and very loving. He and Barbara had known each other long enough to understand each other perfectly.

Even so there were certain problems. One was the McCorquodales, who were very clannish, and after the bitterness of the divorce it was perhaps inevitable that, as Barbara has candidly admitted, 'With the exception of Hugh's mother, I did not like his family and they did not like me.'

Another problem was quite simply over money – and the 'career girl' tendencies from which even Barbara was not entirely immune. As she has written:

My marriage looked like putting an end to my financial worries. My husband was by no means as wealthy as his cousin but he was, until the war altered everything, 'comfortably off'. However, I had decided, during the bitter controversy over my divorce, that I would never again be entirely dependent on anyone. I had learned too how valueless money can be.

In fact this was not very serious. Hugh was a tactful man and not particularly concerned at what she did about the money that her books and journalism brought in. Nor, as the years went by, was Barbara.

And so that autumn as the whole of Britain was caught up in the drama of the Royal abdication and the romance between the King and Mrs Simpson, Barbara was more concerned about another wedding – her own to Hugh. No one outside the family was admitted to the secret but, to her relief, everyone concerned wholeheartedly approved. This time Polly did not ask, 'Darling, is he worthy of you?' as she had with Alexander, for she knew for certain that Hugh was. Raine had known him practically since her birth as her devoted Uncle Hugh and was delighted at the prospect now of having him to live with them.

Inevitably the one person whose reactions Barbara was most concerned about was Ronald. They had been so close so long and meant so much to each other, that it was hard to be completely sure how he would react, despite the fact that he and Hugh had always been extremely fond of each other. She need not have worried. Barbara was spending Christmas on the eve of her marriage with Raine and Polly at Poolbrook. Ronald, already spotted as an up-

and-coming man in politics, had been invited to Trent Park to join the Christmas house-party of the Secretary of State for Air, the wealthy and sophisticated Sir Philip Sassoon, and it was from Trent Park that he wrote to Barbara. The letter reached her on the morning of her marriage.

Darling,

I must send you this morning all my love and thoughts and good wishes for the future. You know what you have meant to me these last five years – much more than I can ever tell you – support, inspiration, courage, faith and love – I've sought them from you often, never in vain. Now, after today, it can't be quite the same – our relationship. But I'm not unhappy about it. I'm glad. Because I *know* you are doing the right thing, the wise thing, and the thing that is going to make you happier and even more lovable to all of us in the future.

Darling, I'd hate you to marry any one but Hugh. I am genuinely delighted that after all this long time you are going to marry him. I can't think of anyone I've met who will look after you and care for you as he will.

Don't ever lose the memory of these last few years; the struggles as well as the victories – and don't forget, darling, all the happy hours we've spent together. I don't think they're finished. There are many more for us in the future. But I want you to know that after them all and because of them I can say you've earned all the love and happiness there is for ever; I know by marrying Hugh that love and happiness will be yours more and more.

Bless you both – always,

R.

The wedding was planned for Monday 28 December, at the Guildhall London, to be followed by a service at St Ethelburgh's Church, Bishopsgate, and a honeymoon in Paris. Hugh spent the Sunday night at his London club, and from there he wrote Barbara a note which she would also open on the morning of the wedding.

My Darling One,

Very soon now you will be my own very darling wife. Oh, my sweet,

I am so wanting the hours to pass quickly till the time we get to Paris and can be alone together. . . .

I feel that I am the luckiest man in the world to be going to be your husband, and though you may be making sacrifices to marry me darling, I will do everything in the world for you to make you happy. . . .

Darling, a little secret. Ever since I really met you properly, I have wanted to marry you and I have never even given a single thought to any other girl. I thought then that you were the loveliest person I had ever seen — now you are more lovely still. To me you are beauty itself, the perfect woman. Darling I am getting older yet you, the loveliest creature God ever made, loves me and wants to marry me. It's so wonderful I can't believe it's true. I fear it may be a dream and I shall wake up and find I was just dreaming of a wonderful fairyland that does not exist at all.

God bless you my angel,

your adoring, Hugh.

One of the problems of the wedding was to avoid publicity, for anything that Barbara did was news. So that Monday morning the legal ceremony at the Guildhall was held early enough to outwit even the hardiest of press photographers, and the only witnesses were Ronald, and Barbara's friend and Hugh's best man, the future Director of Public Prosecutions, Theobald Mathew.

Nothing could have been less romantic than this early morning gathering, but the service afterwards in the tiny Norman Church still decorated with Christmas flowers was very moving. With no one present but Ronald and Theobald Mathew, it was a private, dignified occasion — and from this moment, Barbara says, she knew for certain that this time her marriage would succeed.

Hugh had been planning to start the honeymoon in style by flying to Paris in time for lunch. But Croydon Airport had closed down because of fog, and the bride and bridegroom drove from the Church to Victoria Station hoping that they could still reach Paris on the Golden Arrow. They were lucky. Hugh's company printed for the Southern Railway and because of this the stationmaster found them a compartment of their own on the train to Dover, a private cabin on the ferry, and a *coupé* on the Paris express.

As they left the fog-bound shores of England, it seemed an omen that between them they would overcome the problems that surrounded them and find true married happiness together. Barbara felt the fates were somehow on their side, and as they journeyed on to Paris they were at last 'caught up in an ecstasy which was divinely inspired'. The years of happiness with Hugh had started.

Whenever she talks about her life with Hugh, Barbara is fond of quoting the old remark that 'happiness has no history'. For a while at least it seemed as if the dramas and the struggles of her life were finally behind her and the truth was that her marriage proved the ideal arrangement for her life.

Her feminine side was taken care of now by the devoted Hugh and she was amply cosseted and loved. She explained something of the way she loved him in return in a short article she wrote the following year giving some practical advice to spring brides on dealing with an English husband. Most of it in fact applied to Hugh – and Barbara.

Very often men, although they do not show it, are far more shy than their very modern, self-sufficient wives. This shyness or reserve is actually one of the most charming things about an Englishman . . . and the easiest way to conquer it is to love him deeply – and to show it.

She also offered some more practical advice as well, in which one can catch a glimpse of the energetic Barbara making sure that even on honeymoon Hugh got the exercise he needed.

For your honeymoon, take a pair of comfortable old shoes, and a good warm cardigan. Above all remember that Englishmen need exercise, so let him play his golf, fish and shoot. The husband who is suffering want of exercise is often not a very pleasant companion.

No one stagnates for long with Barbara around, and Hugh enjoyed his shooting and fishing. But one of the great strengths of the marriage was that it never really interfered with Barbara's other interests and activities. She could still write her books and of course could still see Ronald. Despite what he wrote about their relationship never being 'quite the same' after her marriage, nothing had really changed between them. Hugh never wanted to intrude upon the plane of spiritual and intellectual understanding they had shared so long, and now as Ronald's political career began in earnest, Barbara could feel what she had always wanted — that she was still the all-important female influence behind the successful man she loved.

For Ronald *was* successful now, extremely so, and on his own distinctive terms. When he had promised his adoption meeting at King's Norton that he would never be a political weather-vane he spoke truer than most people realised. Even in his maiden speech he had lashed out against his Party's apathy over the chronic unemployed and the so-called 'Distressed Areas'. He had visited South Wales himself — one of the very few Conservative MPs who ever did — and had been appalled by what he saw. Soon he was one of four Conservative MPs who actually voted against the Government for doing nothing about unemployment. He was unpopular among the old men of the Party, but he was already talked about as one of the few MPs with fresh ideas — and the 'only true visionary in the House'.

One of the greatest pleasures of her marriage was that after four years in Half Moon Street, Barbara could finally set up a proper home with Hugh and Raine. Until they could find themselves a house in London, they rented a large ten-roomed flat in Grosvenor Square, and for weekends bought a small thatched cottage by the River Ouse at the village of Great Barford in Bedfordshire. Barbara christened it her 'toy', and they spent countless weekends early in their marriage there. But as they enjoyed the small garden by the river or busied themselves uncovering old beams in its low-ceilinged rooms, neither Hugh nor Barbara realised quite how important the little cottage would be for all of them.

In the meantime, life seemed as busy now for Barbara as it had ever been in the whirlwind years before her marriage. Away from the peace and quiet of Great Barford – which Hugh particularly enjoyed – there was the social life of London. That first summer of their marriage, Barbara and Hugh attended the ball given by the Mountbattens in the spectacular penthouse Edwina had constructed at Brook House in Park Lane, rebuilt since the days when her grandfather used to entertain Edward VII in its marble-pillared splendour.

Barbara was also rapidly caught up again in organising for charity. This time it was a film première in aid of an appeal for journalists' widows and orphans, which Barbara as a journalist herself felt most involved in. She was so involved in fact that, when she realised how little the smart audience had actually contributed, she forthwith berated them from the stage and announced that there were collecting boxes at the doors so that the audience could make amends for their meanness.

Soon afterwards she published what is probably the most untypical of all her novels, *The Forgotten City*, which tells the story of one woman's quest for spiritual truth, and how she finally discovers it within herself – exactly as Barbara had done.

But that autumn even Barbara had to call a temporary halt to her activities. One of her dreams when she had married Hugh had been to have a family, and now suddenly the dream came true. Barbara had the son that she had always longed for. One of her profound beliefs is that the actual act of conception influences the child, and the baby that she now bore seemed to prove her point: just as she had found true physical happiness with Hugh, so the baby was every bit as beautiful as she had wanted. She had willed it to be a boy – and a boy it was. She had also 'prayed and willed him to be brave and clever, to love people and hate injustice'. She called him Ian and, as he grew, his ash-blond hair and perfect features made him look 'so like an angel that I was afraid he would die'.

At the time of Barbara's new-found happiness the family was desperately worried over her brother, Tony. In Cairo he had been thrown from his horse, taken to hospital unconscious, and brought back to England on a stretcher. In March 1937 Polly had been to visit him at the Hospital for Officers at Millbank, and had found him obviously extremely ill. He was barely recognisable as the carefree son that she had known. For the first time in his life he seemed apathetic and depressed, and said that he felt giddy and that his eyes refused to focus properly.

None of the Army doctors seemed much use, despite an angry telephone call from Ronald to Duff Cooper, the Secretary of State for War, complaining that his brother seemed to be scandalously neglected. Rest was prescribed but Tony was obviously as ill as ever, and finally Polly took his case in hand herself. As a good Catholic she had heard about a nursing home in Eastbourne run by a devoted group of nuns. She believed that faith and prayer – as well as rest – were what he needed, and with typical decisiveness soon arranged for Tony to exchange his gloomy bed at Millbank for the peaceful atmosphere of Eastbourne. The nuns were reassuring, telling Polly that they would pray for her son as well as nurse him – and this they did.

The day following his arrival, the local doctor examined Tony and discovered what nobody had realised before: his fall had all but severed the spinal cord at the base of his neck. New treatment was prescribed and before long Tony was on his feet again and ready to return to duty. Tony was grateful to his doctors, but Polly said it proved the power of prayer. Barbara thought that both were right.

Before long Tony was back in Egypt once again, and Barbara had the luck to see him there. Early in 1938 she accompanied her husband on a holiday-cum-business trip visiting the

McCorquodale printing works in the Sudan. They both enjoyed their journey down the Nile – in contrast to the strained circumstances in which Barbara had last made the journey – and when they reached Cairo Tony was there to welcome and make a fuss of them.

There was a whirl of parties, dinners, and sight-seeing trips around the city, but for Barbara much the most important thing about the visit was the chance it gave her to make sure that Tony was completely his old self after his accident.

It was always difficult for outsiders to understand what a devoted family we were – my mother, Ronald, Tony and myself. We were each a part of one another with a feeling of incompleteness when we weren't all together. . . . For us the blood tie was stronger than anything in the world.

Back in England, this same blood tie still ensured that Barbara's life remained irrevocably linked with Ronald's. In Parliament he had done little to endear himself to his Party leaders by continually speaking out against the sufferings of the unemployed. As he cried out in one debate:

I cannot believe that it passes our comprehension and our wit in 1938, with all our inventive power and with this tremendous production and outpouring of wealth, somehow to assure and give to our people a fairer and fuller life, which all deserve but which so few enjoy.

Such words were not expected from Honourable Members on his side of the House, nor was his firm conviction that a war was on its way. It was this conviction that made him one of the small group of Conservative MPs who supported Anthony Eden when he resigned as Foreign Secretary on the issue of appeasement. It also led him to enrol in the Worcestershire and Oxfordshire Yeomanry, and, after his summer camp in the August of 1938, he and Barbara had another brief holiday together. It was to be their last.

Hugh was as understanding as ever – and also anxious to get in a few days' quiet salmon fishing on the Helmsdale, one of the finest salmon rivers in the whole of Scotland. Ian and Raine went off with Polly to the sea, and Barbara and Ronald found themselves a hotel in the pine forest high above the gleaming waters of Lake Brienz, with the snow-capped Jungfrau in the distance.

They followed their customary routine: breakfasting above the lake, reading, walking and discussing everything beneath the sun. Both knew that with the threat of a European war it was unlikely they would ever come again, and Ronald said that he believed the only leader Britain could rely on now was Churchill.

As they returned to England Hitler was massing his troops to invade Czechoslovakia, and a few days later Chamberlain flew to Munich. Ronald was in the House to witness his return with his talk of 'Peace with honour' with the Germans. Describing the applause, Ronald told Barbara, 'I rose very slowly to my feet. I did not cheer.'

Ronald felt miserable and angry at the way the leader of his Party had behaved, and at the hysterical relief in England. Barbara shared his feelings and a few days later at a smart luncheon party had the experience of being told across the table, 'Those traitors – Winston Churchill, your brother, and his like – they should be shot!'

Harold Nicolson recorded, in his diary, Ronald's bitter mood after a dinner they had had with another anti-Chamberlain MP in November 1935: 'Cartland says he cannot stand the Tories any more. He loathes their riches and their self-indulgence. He loathes their mean party schemes. He cannot abide them. . . .' These were sentiments that Barbara shared during that winter of appeasement. And when in the early months of 1939 war appeared increasingly inevitable, she was behind her brother in his passionate support of Churchill, although she privately urged caution.

But Ronald still had one more role to play in the House of Commons, and no one, not even Barbara, would stop him speaking out. It came on 3 August 1939 as Parliament was due to rise for the summer recess. Because of the growing European crisis, Ronald spoke after the Prime Minister to urge an earlier recall of the House. It was refused, and, after accusing Chamberlain of making petty-fogging party speeches, he finished with the dramatic words: 'We are in the situation that within a month we may be going to fight and we may be going to die.'

Harold Nicolson has described what happened then.

At this Patrick Hannon laughs, and Cartland turns upon him with a flame of indignation and says, 'It is all very well for you to laugh. There are thousands of young men at this moment. . . .' The effect is galvanic and I have seldom felt the temperature rise so rapidly.

Afterwards one of Nicolson's friends remarked to him: 'Ronnie Cartland has ruined his chances with the Party but he has made his Parliamentary reputation.'

But the time had come when Parliamentary reputations barely mattered any more.

CHAPTER NINE

Barbara's War

Barbara was six months pregnant and spending August by the sea at Caister, where she and Hugh had rented a house right on the beach. Ian and Raine were with them, and 3 August, the day after Parliament adjourned despite his speech, Ronald arrived to spend a last few days with them, for he knew that he would soon be called up with his Regiment.

He played with the children on the beach, carried blond young Ian pig-a-back upon his shoulders, and seemed quite unconcerned at the storm he had caused in Parliament the day before. It was not until that evening that he told Barbara what had happened – or that he had seriously predicted war within a month. As it happened he was accurate to within a day. On 3 September Germany invaded Poland and war was declared as Ronald knew it would be.

Tony was already with his Regiment back in Britain. Ronald was mobilised as well, and within a few weeks both the brothers were in France, as their father had been twenty-five years earlier. It was hardest now for Polly. She could only pray, and trust that this time her prayers for the safety of her loved-ones would be answered.

Through the beginning of the so-called 'phoney war' Barbara kept in touch with both her brothers. Tony was as cheerful as ever and pretending to be thrilled at the prospect of some real fighting as his best hope of promotion. Ronald had transferred to the Artillery, and would soon be put in charge of an anti-tank battery with the rank of Major. It suited him.

I am in my element, [he wrote to Barbara] complete reorganisation –

office, training, men – everything. It's grand and great fun. The more I think about life the more certain I am that its secret is work – and happy and useful work. I hope Tony won't be disappointed that I got my 'crown' before him. Fantastic in a way when you think that I started the war as a second lieutenant.

That Christmas Barbara's mind was temporarily diverted from worrying about her brothers. Her great friend Mary Cunningham-Reid was now divorced, and she invited Barbara and Hugh and the two children to stay indefinitely with her in the country. Her estate, which she had inherited as a girl from her grandfather, was at Six Mile Bottom just outside Cambridge.

Hugh was delighted, for he was very fond of Mary – she was one of the few outsiders who were allowed to call him Uncle Hugh – and Six Mile Bottom, famous in its day for the shooting parties which were held in honour of King Edward VII, still boasted some of the finest pheasant shooting in the country. Hugh had enjoyed some splendid days there in the past.

On Christmas Day the countryside was under several feet of snow and a few days later, just before midnight on the last day of 1939, Barbara had her baby. Once more she had been praying for a boy, and once again her prayers were answered. It was a big baby and Barbara had a harrowing confinement. But the knowledge that she had a second son made her forget everything but her own and Hugh's excitement.

Barbara had recently written an unusual novel called *The Black Panther* on the theme of reincarnation. (The hero, incidentally, is a portrait of Ronald's friend, the millionaire politician, Sir Philip Sassoon.) And as soon as Barbara saw her new, extremely large and solemn-looking baby, she says that she was 'sure he had been reincarnated many times', and must be what the mystics call, 'an old soul'. She decided she would call him Glen, in memory of one of the great loves of her life.

At this stage of the war, Barbara and Hugh's home was their flat in Grosvenor Square, although they knew if the threatened bombing started, it would be insane to continue in the heart of London with a young family. Already they were making plans to move out permanently to their 'toy cottage' at Great Barford. But shortly after Glen was born they returned to London, and at the beginning of April Barbara had a brief reunion with Ronald.

Parliament had been recalled for one of its important wartime 'secret sessions', and Ronald was summoned back from France for the debate. To Barbara's amazement and delight he suddenly appeared one evening at the flat, wearing civilian clothes and asking if he could stay there for the night. He was excited to be back in London, and as a serving soldier was determined to make a plea in the debate for more guns, better ammunition, more support from the civilians for the fighting. But the debate depressed him. He had no faith in Chamberlain's leadership; Churchill was the only man for him.

Barbara sat up late discussing the war with Ronald. He seemed tired now and fearful for what lay ahead. He talked of the weak line of defence in Belgium and predicted that before long France would fall. Britain would find herself alone against an all-powerful Germany. But the Government would not understand. 'They would rather preserve their dividends and their shooting and fishing weekends, than face the facts which stare them in the face,' he said angrily.

On 12 April Ronald had been planning to go to his constituency to visit his uncle, old Major Howard Cartland, who was still living at The Priory, and in extremely feeble health. He had also planned to be with Polly. But that very morning the headlines showed how justified his fears had been about the enemy advance. The invasion of Belgium he had dreaded had begun.

Birmingham was out. In half an hour he was packed. He had a brief telephone call to Polly. As the boat train had already left, he hired a car to drive him straight to Dover. There was a swift embrace for Barbara, a wave from the car and he was gone. She never saw him again.

It was perfect weather that historic summer of 1940, and Barbara and her family spent it at the cottage. Hugh was running the printing works in London and travelling up each day by train. He was now in his early forties, and his wounds from the First World War, which had left him with one lung, made him medically unfit to fight again. Nor should he have done so much; he was working longer hours than many men half his age, and Barbara worried.

But inevitably what preoccupied her most was the news from France. By May the German armies had advanced through Holland and Belgium. France was cracking and the British Army being pressed inexorably back towards the Channel ports. Ronald and Tony were both caught up in the catastrophe.

There was little news apart from what was in the papers, and Barbara could only talk to Polly on the telephone. In mid-May Ronald found time to write to Polly telling her not to worry if there was a long silence from him now: 'The fog of war is pretty impenetrable.' He said that the weather was lovely, which made him think about her garden and how pretty it must be. He hadn't heard from Tony.

Two days later, Barbara had a letter too from Ronald. Ominously it told her what to do, 'if things don't go right for me'. He ended, 'What a waste it all is – but after months of desolation we shall gain or retain what you and I have always understood the meaning of – freedom.'

This was written from near the Belgian border where Ronald was in action with his battery against heavy German tanks as the retreat continued. After this there were no more letters, from either of the brothers, but the papers were now reporting the beginning of the evacuation of the entire British Army from the beaches of Dunkirk. Polly and Barbara hoped and waited, as the first of the British troops reached England.

But there was no news until 6 June. Then Polly received two telegrams. They were almost identical and both were signed by the Secretary of State for War.

Regret to inform you that Major J.R.H. Cartland MP, RA is missing, further particulars will be forwarded as soon as possible.

Regret to inform you that Captain J.A.H.Cartland, the Lincolnshire Regiment, is reported by his Unit as missing, further particulars will be forwarded as soon as possible.

Polly knew quite well the anguish that would follow now, the days of interminable waiting, the longing for news – any news. For she had been through it all before in those cruel months in 1918 when her husband Bertie was reported missing too. It was always the uncertainty which proved hardest in the end to bear and finally one longed for any news – even the worst – rather than the agony of waiting.

Polly was rock-like. She had her prayers, her faith to sustain her – and besides, she believed well-bred people did not break down in public. It was not done and the boys would not have liked it. Barbara did her best to follow her example, and they telephoned each other every day on the off-chance that one or other might have heard something. Neither had. They comforted each other, but the one thing Barbara did not tell her mother was the dream she had the night the telegrams arrived.

It had been a horrifying dream. She had seen Ronald standing, looking very pale. She spoke to him and he did not reply, and then she saw in the centre of his forehead a neat round bullet-hole. After this dream she was certain that he must be dead.

She tried remembering the conversation she and Ronald had so many times about the after-life. Death, he had always said, was very unimportant. Mirroring his thoughts, she herself had written of how,

a very strong personality often leaves this life before wearing out his body. 'Those whom the Gods love die young,' said the Greeks. We say, 'those who have advanced enough'. . . Like a balloon which cannot be held down by a slender string, they snap the bodily cord which holds them, and go. They have progressed to the spirtual level to be merged into the fourth dimension, there to advance still further on the path to divinity.

Barbara believed that this had happened with her brother, but it did not make the waiting any easier. Hugh was the most comforting and understanding of human beings, but even to him it was impossible to explain the gaping sense of loss. It was now high summer and the perfect days continued. The lilac faded and the garden bloomed beside the gentle flowing river. The children played and were oblivious of the war.

But Ronald was everywhere. He had helped to paint the windows of the cottage and to plant the garden. 'I kept expecting to hear him come into the room, to hear him say, "What *do* you think, darling . . . ?" to meet him striding round the corner in his old quick, unhesitating manner.'

She also felt the inevitable misery of regret. 'An unkind word; a needless criticism; times when I had been too busy; letters which had not been written; presents which had not been given.'

Was there any hell, she asked herself, like the hell of regretting when it was too late?

Luckily for Barbara she had little time to brood. The Battle of Britain had just started and Hugh, in addition to his work in London, was training a detachment of the local Home Guard. With the bombing starting Hugh and Barbara's chief fears were naturally for the children now, and there were already rumours that because of the invasion scare, the Government was planning to evacuate women and children from the South.

In the midst of all this, Barbara was rung up by her old friend, Lady Dunn. They had remained close friends since she had married Sir James after that disastrous trip to Deauville more than ten years earlier. Sir James was still the intimate confidant of Beaverbrook, who had just joined the new Churchill Government, and the word from him was that Churchill himself was now convinced the Germans would invade. There were official plans for a mass evacuation of women and children to Canada. She was going with her children and her husband had just telephoned suggesting Barbara and her young should go with them as well. They had a spare cabin on the ship, and the Dunns would look after them in Canada. She must decide at once.

It was a difficult decision. Barbara's instincts were to stay with Hugh. She felt he needed her, and whatever her failings, cowardice is not among them. On the other hand there was undoubtedly her duty to her children. Glen was barely six months old, and there were horrifying stories in the press of the effect of bomb blast on tiny babies. Hugh was also anxious for their safety and did his best to persuade her to accept. Against her better judgement she finally agreed. 'It was,' she says, 'a terrible mistake.'

At the end of June they sailed from Tilbury in one of the big Canadian Pacific liners, the *Duchess of Atholl*. It was crowded and there were not enough life boats for the 1,300 children aboard, let alone the adults. From the start Barbara was uneasy at the thought that all the families around her were the better-off, and many of them very rich indeed.

Apart from Lady Dunn and her children, there was Lady Carnarvon, the former Tilly Losch, the American-born Lady Jersey, and Somerset Maugham's daughter, Liza Paravicini, who secretly infuriated Barbara by her extraordinary composure and the way she spent the voyage on deck reading Tolstoy's *War and Peace* without 'one of her smooth, shining golden hairs ever out of place'.

Barbara was already very much aware of the young families in Ronald's old constituency of King's Norton. They had been left behind and Barbara, whatever her excuses, was enjoying the privileges of the rich. Ronald would never have approved of that.

When they reached Montreal her uneasiness continued. The Canadians were hospitable and sympathetic, but she missed

England more than she had ever thought possible. She missed Hugh, and there was still no news of either of her brothers. Money was short because she had not been allowed to bring enough from Britain. And to make her more uneasy still, she soon heard that the British Government had changed its mind and was definitely not evacuating Southern England nor any more children as had been intended. As she read the news of the Battle of Britain, she had the feeling now that she was missing Britain's finest hour.

The Dunns took her and the children to a smart resort called Metis Beach which reminded Barbara of a 'paler version of Bembridge in the Isle of Wight'. She felt run down and wretched. She had accepted now that both her brothers must be dead, and the full impact of what had happened finally hit her. Raine and Ian developed measles in the hotel and had to be kept hidden. Under Canadian law they should have been taken to a fever hospital.

There was no one she could talk to. The kind Canadians continued to ask her how she liked their country – and she continued to reply that it was lovely. But she had reached rock bottom and was suddenly struck with absolute unreasoning despair. It was totally unlike her – and all the more frightening because of it. 'I felt trapped and desperate, helpless and utterly despondent,' she wrote later.

These few weeks in Canada at Metis Beach marked the lowest point of Barbara's life: it was rather like a repetition of her loneliest period after her divorce – only infinitely worse. But once again she knew there was no point feeling sorry for herself. And once again she found her recovery in the surest therapy of all – hard work.

She wrote some articles on her experiences. She did two lecture-tours in Lower Canada speaking on Britain and the war. And she managed once they were in Montreal to make some money – which she and the children badly needed – by accepting a commission from a millionaire to write the story of his life. His

name was Philip Saunders and he had invented the Saunders
Valve. Although she did the book in record time and received her
fee, a very welcome £250, to this day it remains the only Barbara
Cartland book that has never been published.

Now that she was facing life again, Barbara had come to a
decision. Since the trip to Canada had been such a hideous mistake,
there was only one thing to be done – return to Britain, and as soon
as possible.

It was September, with the Battle of Britain at its height, but as
she wrote, 'If the great majority of children in Great Britain could
stand up to bombing, mine could too; one need not be foolhardy,
but one could be there . . . one with other wives and mothers . . .
fighting side by side.'

Poor Hugh was instantly bombarded with a stream of Barbara's
telegrams and letters asking him to get them home. He replied that
this was difficult as Barbara had agreed in writing to stay in
Canada a minimum of six months. This made no difference, she
replied. She was coming back, whatever happened, and she
suggested people he should ask to make it possible: Ronald's old
friend, Anthony Eden; the Canadian Minister in London,
Vincent Massey; Leo Amery; the head of every shipping line.
'If necessary, contact the Prime Minister himself,' she cabled.

In fact it was Barbara who finally obtained a Canadian
Government permit to return, by pleading with an influential
Canadian businessman whom she had met. Even then they had to
wait until the beginning of November when there was a ship from
Montreal. And by then the Allied shipping losses in the North
Atlantic had increased dramatically. The U-boat war was hotting
up, and German battleships were preying on our shipping.

A cable now arrived from Hugh: 'Very concerned increased sea
dangers. Think advisable postpone return for a month.' James
Dunn added his weight to Hugh's advice. The risk, he said, was far
too great. One or two more candid friends told Barbara she was a

'murderess' to think of exposing her children to such frightful dangers.

She admits that even she was slightly shaken by the reaction – and as sailing day drew near began having nightmares that Ian was drowning. As always at a time of great decision, Barbara prayed for guidance, and something made her open her Bible at random. Eyes shut, she put her finger on the page and when she looked saw she had picked the following verse: 'And there went a proclamation throughout the host about the going down of the sun, saying "Every man to his city and every man to his own country!"'

The decision had been taken for her and on 14 November, in the middle of the first blizzard of the winter, Barbara and the children boarded the Canadian Pacific ship *Duchess of Richmond*, and sailed for England.

Most of the other passengers aboard the ship were the first Commonwealth air-crews returning to Britain after training in Canada. They were a light-hearted lot, enjoying their first relaxation after months of intensive training. But despite their presence, it was a fearsome voyage. The ship was on her own, relying on her speed to outrun the enemy and so do without protection from a convoy. And she was virtually unarmed. Ian developed the beginnings of pneumonia. Barbara found it difficult to sleep.

They had reached mid-Atlantic when in the middle of the night Barbara heard a terrific bang, and thought, 'Now we're for it!' She leapt from her bunk, grabbed Ian's snow-suit, and was just about to wake him when she realised the ship was curiously quiet. There was no shouting, no alarm-bells. The bang that she had heard must have been a door slamming in the corridor.

But as she stood there in the middle of the night in the silent ship with nothing but the faint throb of the engines far below, she was suddenly gripped by terror, a mindless panic that she and the children were trapped there in the liner, in the middle of the ocean, with nobody to save them.

She has no idea how long the terror lasted. It seemed an age. Then suddenly it lifted, for she knew that she was not alone. Someone was with her, 'Not Ronald, but someone I had once loved and who had loved me. ' Glen Kidston had perished nearly ten years before when his aircraft hit that hill in Africa, but now,

He was there as surely as if I could see and hear him. He was beside me, as real and as unchanged in our relationship to each other as he had been when I had last seen him. I was no longer afraid, and I knew with an unshakeable conviction that he had come to take us into port. I fell asleep, but he was still there in the morning and for the rest of the voyage. Only when we sighted the coast of England did he go as swiftly as he had come, and I have never been close to him since.

Barbara has never attempted to explain how this occurred, contenting herself with the thought that there are things that happen which defy explanation by our limited human intelligence. But she is convinced that during the second-half of her voyage Glen Kidston was beside her, and that in some way the presence of this man she had loved had helped to bring her safely back to England.

Just a few hours after Kidston left her, she and the excited children were disembarking on the docks at Liverpool, and Hugh was there to hold her in his arms.

After the safety and the leisured luxury of Canada, it was an abrupt change to find herself cramped with the children into the tiny cottage at Great Barford. The war had now begun in earnest and almost everything was in short supply, but she was happier than she had been for months.

The flat in Grosvenor Square was let, and life in the cottage seemed chaotic after the ordered elegance they had known before. Books were piled everywhere. Toys, dogs and cats and children seemed to fill every square inch of the shabby little house, and the only touch of order came from some framed sporting-prints of Hugh's which he had hung in the dining-room. But Barbara was back where she belonged. The wretched months of exile were behind her.

She was still haunted by the cruel uncertainty about her brothers. Officially they were still no more than 'missing', but she was coming to accept the fact that she would never see either of them again. So was Polly, although she still clung desperately to the hope that one of them at least might still be surviving in a German prison camp.

Then at the beginning of 1941, they learned the truth. It was confirmed officially that Tony had died most gallantly refusing to surrender when surrounded by advancing Germans. And soon afterwards they received a letter from a brother-officer of Ronald's now in a prisoner-of-war camp. He had seen him killed. Ronald had been leading his men towards the Dunkirk beaches when German tanks converged on them. A bullet struck him in the forehead, exactly as in Barbara's dream. He had died instantly, the first Member of Parliament to be killed in action in the war.

At least the waiting and uncertainty were over now, and the tributes that flowed in to Ronald's memory, helped a little, as tributes do. One of the most moving testimonials to the future that had lain before him came from Anthony Eden who wrote, 'We were all so sure that he had a great part to play in the world after the war, for he had the true qualities of leadership, vision, courage and faith. Of all the younger men I knew, his was the fairest future.'

'The fairest future!' As Barbara read this she could not help remembering her brother on that night so many years before when they had come to London, and he had boasted, 'I shall be Prime Minister.' Could anything justify the waste of war?

That night Barbara dreamed again of Ronald. He was no longer wounded, but full of his old vitality and life, and Barbara had

Barbara as Lady Castlemaine at the Famous Beauties Ball

Ronald Cartland, Barbara's elder brother, a visionary and brilliant young politician. He was the first MP to be killed in World War II, at Dunkirk on 30 May 1940. Barbara's biography of him, written in 1942, had a preface by Sir Winston Churchill

Anthony Cartland, Barbara's younger brother, in the Lincolnshire Regiment. When the Germans asked him to surrender he replied, 'I will surrender only unto God.' He was killed at Dunkirk on 29 May 1940, and was given a posthumous award for gallantry

Barbara with Raine, her two sons, Ian and Glen, and Wong. As a Voluntary Junior Commander (Captain) in the ATS, she was Chief Lady Welfare Officer to the Armed Services in Bedfordshire

Barbara with the Countess Mountbatten of Burma, looking at the St John Ambulance Brigade Exhibition which she organised. It toured the country and made £50,000 for local funds

Barbara's daughter Raine as Débutante of the Year, 1947, in the dress which required no coupons

Darling mummy with all my love Raine 1947

Raine's wedding in 1948 to Gerald Legge, later the Earl of Dartmouth. She wore the same dress with orange blossom added

Barbara with her second husband (Hugh), Ian and Glen at the Park Gates of Camfield Place

Barbara's elder son, Ian, who is now her Manager

Barbara's unmarried son, Glen, a stockbroker, who listens to all her manuscripts and travels with her round the world

Barbara opening a Health Shop. She is President of the National Association for Health and answers 10,000 letters on health every year. She has no financial interest in anything she recommends

Barbara and her white Rolls-Royce, BC 29, the first white Rolls ever made for England by Jack Barclay. Barbara calls it her Trade Mark

Barbara today. At seventy-eight she has recently celebrated the sale of her one hundredth million book, recorded an album of love songs with the Royal Philharmonic Orchestra, and had her novel, *The Flame is Love* filmed

rushed up to him, saying, 'Darling, you are alive! I knew you
were, how wonderful!' She had gone on to tell him how amused
he'd be to read all the nice things people had said about him when
they thought that he was dead. He laughed at that and Barbara was
full of an extraordinary happiness. Then she awoke.

It was a bitter awakening, and to preserve the memory of that
happiest of dreams, she wrote a poem which she called, 'Alive'.

> I dreamt last night of you,
> It was so real, so true, I knew
> You lived – although they said
> You were dead.
>
> I dreamed you kissed me, then
> We laughed just as we did when
> You were here – before they said
> That you were dead.
>
> I know you are alive
> I cannot see you but you are beside
> Me still, as you were before they said –
> So stupidly – that you were dead.

From that moment Barbara has never really felt herself apart
from Ronald, but she knew that the last thing he would want
would be for her to live a life of mourning, and soon after this she
looked around to see what war work she could do. She began in
the WVS, organising the distribution of books and magazines to
the different camps throughout the country. Before long, as with
almost everything that Barbara undertakes, the work had
snowballed, and she found herself with an honorary commission
in the ATS and working as a full-time Welfare Officer responsible
for the well-being of all the Armed Services in Bedfordshire and
especially the women's.

It was a demanding job, for Bedfordshire had several vital and
top-secret Airforce bases and the women serving there inevitably
found themselves lonely, bored and cut off from the world outside.

Until Barbara came along little had been done to keep them happy
and she applied her imagination and energy to the task.

Apart from trying to organise some social life for them, it was
typical of Barbara to insist on bringing some colour into their
surroundings: some of the dingiest rest rooms and even the
operational ones were soon transformed with the walls painted in
authentic Cartland colours – flame pink and her favourite Nile
blue. 'Most of them,' she said, 'were soon far more colourful and
cheerful than the rooms we had at the cottage.'

It was another typical Barbara touch to start wondering what to
do for the girls who were planning wartime marriages. Most of
these weddings were inevitably rushed and drab affairs, the exact
opposite of the sort of glamorous romantic weddings Barbara
believed that every woman ought to have. But with only twelve
clothing coupons a year, it was impossible for these war brides to
buy themselves a wedding-dress, even if they could have afforded
it on their Service pay.

As she toured the Airforce camps, Barbara found girls actually
in tears, saying they *had* to be married in white – otherwise they'd
not feel '*properly* married'. On their behalf Barbara tried tackling
the heads of the women's forces at the War Office. She asked for
extra clothing coupons for Service brides, only to get the blankest
of blank refusals from those formidable female Generals.

Resourceful as ever, Barbara decided it must be possible to get
second-hand dresses if new ones were not available. As when hard
up in the past she had bought second-hand dresses for herself, she
advertised in *The Lady* and bought two near-perfect dresses for
seven and eight pounds each. These she sent to the War Office
with her compliments and a note suggesting that Service brides
might borrow them for the day and return them afterwards.

Rather to her surprise, the idea was enthusiastically received,
and soon Barbara, in addition to her other duties, had the task of
buying and dispatching wedding-dresses for all three of the

women's Services. By the end of the war Barbara had purchased over a thousand dresses, and all of them had been ironed, packed and then dispatched from the cottage at Great Barford.

It was through her welfare work that Barbara now came in contact with one of the very few women she unreservedly admires. Being such a close friend of Mary Cunningham-Reid, it was inevitable that she should have got to know well and love her more famous sister, Lord Louis Mountbatten's wife, Edwina. She had been to the fabulous parties the Mountbattens held at Brook House in Park Lane before the war and had admired Edwina as the most glamorous and envied beauty and social figure of the era.

But now with the war, the Mountbattens had taken on a new and legendary role. Lord Louis, after heroic service in command of the destroyer, HMS *Kelly*, was in charge of Combined Operations, and his wife was head of the all-important St John Ambulance Brigade. This voluntary service had borne the brunt of succouring the injured in the Blitz, and Edwina Mountbatten with her bravery and tireless activity had become an inspiration wherever the need was greatest.

In February 1943, Barbara invited her to come and speak to the WAAF personnel at the nearby RAF Aerodrome at Cardington. Her talk was a great success, for Edwina was a clever and amusing speaker and she spent the night with Barbara at Great Barford. It was through this visit that Barbara first became interested in the St John Ambulance Brigade. Its romantic history – it traced itself back to the First Crusade – naturally appealed to her, and when she was told of the need for someone to organise the St John cadets in Bedfordshire, she took on the job, in addition to her other duties.

Hugh tried to make her slow down, but this was one thing she could never do, and before long the unstoppable Barbara had recruited over two thousand young cadets in the County, and was soon organising a Cadet Revue, a camp, and countless new

activities to keep them busy. In collaboration with a friend, Joyce
Camden, she wrote them their own marching song, which was
adopted by the St John cadets throughout the world.

And so the war years passed in this frenzy of activity; yet
Barbara still found time to be with her family and to write books
like: *The Dark Stream* whose hero was an artist working on
camouflage for the RAF; *After the Night*, described as 'a novel of
drama, passion and intrigue'; *Open Wings*, a story of the RAF; and
Out of Reach, with its beautiful young heroine paralysed from a
hunting accident, but managing to keep the love of an unfaithful
husband.

Throughout this period the work which gave Barbara her
greatest satisfaction was the biography she wrote of Ronald. This
was one book she did not dictate, but believes it was dictated to
her. It remains her proudest literary achievement. Nothing would
bring her brother back, but he still lives in this moving, very
simple account of his short and happy life. Now he would never be
forgotten, and the praise of the critics came as a tribute to his
memory.

One of the most distinguished of them, Raymond Mortimer,
called Ronald's life, 'a crusade of moral bravery'. But for Barbara
the words that inevitably pleased her most came from the Preface
Winston Churchill wrote for the book.

Ronald Cartland was a man of noble spirit, who followed his
convictions without thought of personal advancement. At a time when
our political life had become feckless and dull, he spoke fearlessly for
Britain. His words and acts were instinct with the sense of our country's
traditions and duty. His courage and bearing inspired those who met or
heard him.

It is a fitting tribute from the statesman Ronald most admired; and
as for Barbara she says that even now not a day goes by without her
thinking of her brother as a living presence in her life.

CHAPTER TEN

Public Figures

Not long before he died, Ronald described the war as, 'a tremendous opportunity — a colossal mental jerk for which we should be deeply grateful'.

Certainly it had been so far for Barbara. She had been organising people, taking decisions and working for a purpose greater than herself. And now that peace had come there was inevitably something of a gap. It would have all been very different had Ronald only been alive, for as his political career progressed, Barbara would have been able to continue with her longed-for role — that of the woman who achieves her life's ambition by inspiring and supporting the man she loves. But with Ronald gone and the war over, the powerful, crusading side of Barbara's nature was rather left without a purpose.

Hugh gave her all the cosseting and married happiness she needed but, as he would have been the first to have admitted, he was no substitute for Ronald. Five days a week he was managing the printing business, and at weekends he enjoyed relaxing in the cottage at Great Barford. He loved his home, his garden and his children. Most of all, he still doted on his wife, as he showed in the short note he wrote her on their wedding anniversary the year the war in Europe ended.

My Own Darling Wife,
I love you more and more as the years go by. . . .
I shall be thinking of my darling wife all day and how lucky I was nine years ago when you married me.
Bless you, my beautiful sweetheart,
Your adoring,
Hugh.

Barbara knew all too well that she was lucky too, and realised that Hugh needed careful looking after. He was extraordinarily resilient, but his chest wounds from the First World War – and the strains and worries of the Second – had left him vulnerable, and Barbara was determined he should receive all the love and care and nourishment he needed.

And obviously the children needed her as well. Ian was eight, his brother Glen was five, and Raine, now nearly seventeen, was increasingly dependent on her mother. The time had come for Barbara to concentrate her energies on her family, and although she was approached by two Constituencies to represent them politically, she reluctantly refused them both, replying that she had three young children : 'In looking after them I am doing work of National Importance, for the future depends on them. My place is in the home.'

An intriguing mother-and-daughter situation had now emerged between Barbara and her daughter, Raine. For things had changed considerably from those early days in Half Moon Street when Barbara, recently divorced, had been so desperately concerned to bring her up herself. Throughout those early years, Barbara had always tried to be the sort of mother towards Raine that Polly had been to her. But then – what with remarriage and the war – this had become steadily more difficult.

Barbara had had her war work, and there was not that same desperate sense of 'all of us against the world' which had bound Polly to her children after Bertie died. Her Uncle Hugh was the gentlest of stepfathers to Raine, but she admits that once she began mixing with other girls, it upset her that she seemed to be the only one whose parents were divorced.

After the return from Canada, Barbara and Hugh had sent her to a nearby school, which by chance had turned out to be 'the most fashionable girls' school in England', evacuated to a Stately Home a few miles from the cottage. Other girls from various wealthy families she met here invited her home for holidays and she had grown to dislike living in the cottage which seemed poky and uncomfortable compared with the grander homes of the richer girls that she visited.

On the other hand, she was devoted to Polly. Since she was very young, she had been spending holidays with her at Poolbrook. They got on splendidly together, and Raine had naturally absorbed many of Polly's attitudes to life.

Academically Raine was extremely bright, and for a period Barbara, to her horror, began to think she had produced a teenage blue-stocking, quite devoid of dress-sense or awareness of her looks. This caused inevitable arguments. 'Do tidy your hair, and clean your face, darling,' Barbara would exclaim. 'No man wants a clever woman!'

And it was usually left to Hugh to calm things down by reassuring Barbara that this was 'just a stage' which Raine would soon grow out of. Which of course Raine did – thanks largely to Barbara's efforts.

For the ending of the war coincided with the period when Raine – with excellent School Certificate results behind her now – left her smart boarding school for a finishing school in Sussex. She was now sixteen, and Barbara decided that the time had come to take her daughter firmly in hand.

She had perfect features and a lovely figure, so I decided I was going to produce her as a beauty. She was still going through a very scruffy period, and at times I really used to bully her and become absolutely furious with her – as I suppose mothers often do with daughters. Hugh used to tell me, 'You're being beastly to poor Raine,' but of course the bullying worked, and soon she was starting to make the most of herself, which was really all that mattered.

Polly had originally inspired Barbara to succeed in life, and it was now that Barbara set out to do the same for Raine. As a young girl in her early teens, Raine had been somewhat shy: Barbara cured her of this by teaching her to speak in public and project herself.

I used to get her to make a speech to me, rather as Ronald used to do, and while she was speaking I'd go into the room next door and shout, 'I can't hear you. Speak more clearly.' I was delighted when she later won the gold medal for elocution at the London Academy of Music and Dramatic Art.

The urge towards success did not end there. By 1947 Raine was due to 'come out' as a débutante in the spring, and since the social roundabout had started up again after the war, the ballrooms and the garden parties were once again in full swing.

Things had changed a lot from the spacious days when Polly had presented Barbara as débutante at Court, looking very splendid in a purple and sequined creation by young Norman Hartnell in 1925. Clothes were still on coupons, and there was a widespread feeling that the whole system of presenting débutantes at Court had outlived its usefulness – a feeling which the Royal Family must have shared when they abolished the presentations just a few years later.

Barbara herself admitted this in an article she wrote that summer. 'Let us be frank,' she wrote, 'débutantes, unless they are your own particular property, are bores!'

But as a débutante, Raine still counted as Barbara's 'own particular property' – and it was typical of Barbara to insist that since her daughter *was* a débutante, she should become the most successful one of all. That spring, much of Barbara's energy – and her extraordinary powers of promotion – went into making sure she was.

Inevitably Raine's dresses played a big part in this, and there were all the problems associated with clothes' rationing. But Barbara had more experience than most mothers at coping with them. Not for nothing had she dressed herself fashionably on a very small budget in the Twenties and found all those wedding-dresses for her Service brides in the war.

That April for Raine's début at the Queen Charlotte Ball, Barbara commissioned Worth to copy a dress originally worn by the Empress Eugénie and make it up in yards of white tulle she had brought back from a brief holiday in Switzerland. It was still impossible to buy such materials in England. She used even greater ingenuity for some of Raine's other dresses.

One of Barbara's friends produced a crinoline, which formed the basis of several of Raine's most memorable dresses. As Barbara wrote,

We had to think up all sorts of different ways of making Raine look striking. Artificial flowers were free of coupons; we bought a big wreath of daisies, poppies and cornflowers and sewed it round the neck of a dress of blue taffeta which she had bought at school from a friend for £3, adding a wide, velvet hem. Over the crinoline it looked lovely, and the American Ambassador said it was one of the prettiest dresses he had seen in London.

Barbara herself designed another of Raine's dresses – green tulle with pink roses at each shoulder – which was photographed incessantly. It amused her when she heard other mothers say how difficult it was to clothe their daughters elegantly, and remembered just how little she had spent on Raine.

Even Raine's presentation dress was a 1934 vintage Molyneux model which Barbara spotted in a second-hand dress shop in South Molton Street. Raine told one reporter that she was slightly scared that it might split when she curtseyed – but it didn't.

Nor were clothes all that mattered. After that 'scruffy' early teenage period, Barbara could now write that 'one of the most outstanding things about her was that she was so neat and tidy'.

She had not one but three dances given in her honour: the first by Barbara and Hugh; the second by an old friend and MP for

South Bedfordshire Alan Lennox-Boyd; and the third by one of Barbara's oldest friends and Raine's godfather, the Duke of Sutherland, at Sutton Place, his Elizabethan house near Guildford (later famous as the English home of Paul Getty).

Raine was asked everywhere and featured in all the papers and the social magazines. Typical of the write-ups she received was the following caption to a full-page photograph in the *Leader* magazine.

Eighteen years old with a face the shape of a heart, Miss Raine McCorquodale turns dancing eyes upon the world. Eternally smiling — at Ascot, in Bond Street, at dances and at parties, she reminds us of another age, when there were courts in Europe, when a girl 'came out' in a recognised manner, and one of them was hailed as the Toast of the Town.

For in consciously 'producing' her daughter as a beauty, Barbara had in fact created Raine in the image of one of the virgin heroines of one of her later novels. And it was not entirely a matter of coincidence that at this very moment when Raine was reminding people of some acknowledged beauty of the past, Barbara herself should have turned her literary attention to another age.

Until now all her romantic novels had been set in the present day, but as she admitted in an interview in the United States *Globe and Mail*,

You can't dress your heroine up, because clothes are rationed. You can't give her a glamorous occupation because labour is directed. You can't describe a dinner party because food is rationed. You can't even send her for a ride in a car, because there is no petrol. So I'm escaping to the past and writing a novel about the Regency.

It was called *The Hazard of Hearts* and featured the very first of Barbara's historical romantic virgins, who in dress, in style, in clear-eyed, youthful glamour had an extraordinary resemblance to Raine.

During her season Raine herself confirmed her accolade as 'toast of the town' being voted 'Débutante of the Year' — the prettiest, most popular, most talked-about and written-about girl in London. She had succeeded — as both Polly and her mother had told her that she should — and to complete the full scenario of a Barbara Cartland novel, she now fell romantically in love.

In 1947, just before the season started, she had been skiing in Switzerland and had met a young man from the City called Gerald Legge. He was charming, rich and the eldest son of the heir presumptive to the Earl of Dartmouth. In January 1948, when Barbara and Hugh were on a business trip to the United States (Barbara was officially representing British authors to American publishers), they had a telegram informing them of Raine's engagement.

It was all most romantic, a copybook conclusion to a Barbara Cartland novel, but Barbara had to admit that in real life she was, not particularly pleased, for although I liked Gerald very much, I thought Raine was too young. . . . She was only eighteen, she had not seen much life, and as she was very pretty it seemed rather absurd to rush into marriage until she had had a good look round to make quite certain Gerald was the right man.

Inevitably, Barbara's words of caution had not the least effect, and in June 1948 Raine, like Barbara twenty years before her, walked up the aisle of St Margaret's Westminster. Nineteen-year-old Raine McCorquodale had now become Mrs Gerald Legge.

Soon after the war, Hugh and Barbara had bought a large house in South Street, Mayfair, and throughout the period of Raine's début it had been ideal. But now that Raine was off their hands, neither of them really wanted to live in the heart of London any more. They both longed to settle permanently in the country. The cottage at Great Barford was obviously too small for them now that the boys were growing up, and Barbara had still not got those 'Park Gates' of her very own.

The problem was to find a suitable country place still close

enough to London to allow Hugh to travel to the office every day.
They began looking to the north of London – where one can still
reach open countryside much quicker than to the south – and at the
beginning of 1950, Barbara heard that Camfield Place was empty.

It had belonged to the late Lord Queenborough, but what
naturally caught Barbara's imagination was that Beatrix Potter
stayed here as a girl: Peter Rabbit and his friends had lived in the
woods belonging to the house, and the kitchen garden had not
changed since Peter Rabbit raided it for Mr McGregor's soporific
lettuces.

The house seemed vast and run down and dilapidated. Hugh
thought it far too much to cope with, but Barbara with her usual
gusto saw it as another challenge and soon persuaded him to buy it.
It proved a great success. Barbara had read how Beatrix Potter as a
girl had felt that the house was haunted – and so, rather than take
any chances, she had it blessed by the local Rector. It was a
precaution to which Barbara ascribes the house's 'happy and
peaceful atmosphere'.

More to the point, perhaps, she soon set about painting and
furnishing it in her own inimitable style. In place of the old
discoloured walls and gloomy corridors there was soon Nile Blue
and Cartland Pink. It was the first time Barbara had been able to
carry out her decorative schemes on the scale that she had dreamed
of – and they turned out to be extraordinarily successful.

The house became her hobby. Junk shops were ransacked for
four-poster beds, paintings were purchased at what now seem
bargain prices, and gradually Camfield Place began to come to
life. It had always needed colour, and this was what Barbara gave
it now. Before long Camfield Place became what it has been ever
since – a glamorous version of a traditional English country house.
It suited all the family. When the boys went to Harrow, like their
father, the school was barely half an hour away. Barbara could
write her books in peace, and Hugh could shoot across the land.

For a while they even had a prize dairy herd, with the cows named after the heroines from Barbara's novels.

Looking back, Barbara picks on this period as her time of greatest tranquillity and happiness, the nearest to a time of pure contentment she has ever known. But even then the Cartland energy would not let her gently relax. She needed challenges, activity, and the feeling she was doing things for people as Polly had always taught her that she should. The crusading Barbara Cartland was soon on the move again.

'It doesn't matter terribly what a wife does during the day provided she is always home at six o'clock to greet her husband properly when he returns from work.'

Throughout her married life, Barbara always did her best to stick by her own advice on how to keep a husband happy. Nothing was allowed to impinge upon the time she spent with Hugh, and she found that as the years went by their love was deepening and steadily improving.

'To be happily married,' she has written, 'you must "think happiness"' – and not rely on some magical romantic happy ending to sustain you ever after. She and Hugh 'thought happiness' with great success throughout their life together and once a year went off to Paris for a second honeymoon. 'Darling,' she used to say to him, 'in twenty-seven years of marriage, you have often annoyed, irritated and infuriated me, but my darling, you have never bored me.'

Nor did she allow boredom to invade her life when Hugh was at the office. Producing three books a year took only part of every day – before Hugh returned at six o'clock – and these early post-war years became a time of considerable achievement.

Her one great interest which had continued from the war was the St John Ambulance Brigade and she had organised a travelling exhibition for St John's, which was opened by the Queen and

earned over £50,000 for the local Divisions. Still inspired by
Edwina Mountbatten's example, Barbara now became Vice-
President of the St John's Cadets in Hertfordshire.

Then in 1955, because she believed it was what Ronald would
wish her to do, Barbara now stood for the Hertfordshire County
Council, and was elected, after waging a typically colourful
campaign, in what had always previously been a strongly-held
Labour seat. By now Raine had entered local politics herself — as an
outspoken and publicity conscious member of the Westminster
City Council — and the two of them made an impressive mother-
and-daughter team.

In some ways Raine was very like her mother as a public figure,
and had clearly inherited much of Barbara's flair for combining
glamour with the effective public gesture. 'Publicity?' she once
admitted to a journalist, in the very words that Barbara might have
used. 'Of course I've chased it. I admit it openly. But I am not
interested in politics or publicity for its own sake, but as a way of
getting things done.'

Raine had a great deal of her mother's impatience with
sloppiness or unnecessary inefficiency: her best-remembered coup
was her splendid outburst against filthy crockery at London
Airport. But her most important work was propably the campaign
which she and Barbara waged together to improve the treatment
of Britain's aged.

This began when Barbara, as a Hertfordshire County
Councillor, visited a nearby home for old women in Hatfield. By
now she had already shaken up the Council — to considerable
effect. Like Raine she was interested, not in politics or publicity as
such, but in getting things done, and she says that her fellow
Councillors were already treating her 'like a bomb which might
explode at any moment'.

And explode she duly did after she had seen the old women's
home. For what she found was seventy-two old ladies crammed
into a former workhouse with capacity for less than half that

number. Their beds were a foot apart, they had nowhere to put their personal belongings, and they were just waiting for death.

Barbara went into action. There was an enormous rumpus, followed by official denials, secret investigations, and barristers brought in to answer Barbara's accusations. Many would have retired defeated, but Barbara is not easily overawed. She is a powerful campaigner, and since the early Fifties had been writing a weekly column of her own in the *Sunday Dispatch* – under the heading, 'Barbara Cartland, the Woman Who Sets the World Talking'.

She certainly did now: 'If dogs were treated in this country, *as old folk are*,' she wrote, 'there would immediately be a national outcry!'

The national outcry quickly followed. Barbara was soon visiting all the other old peoples' homes in the County and reporting what she found. Raine took up the cause, and visited more than 250 homes throughout the country. The Government announced an 'Inquiry into the Housing and Conditions of Old People', and while Barbara soon made sure that things were rectified in Hertfordshire, the report that she and Raine prepared finally formed the basis of official legislation. This was the one crusade of Barbara's that Hugh disliked because it upset her so. The more homes she discovered, where old men and women were neglected, badly fed and bullied, the more she reacted to their sufferings. Hugh protective as ever begged her not to take it so much to heart. But until she got the County Council alerted to what was happening and the homes improved she had many sleepless nights.

Other campaigns followed; one was for better salaries for nurses and midwives and another – the most difficult of her whole career – concerned the gypsies. Barbara discovered that 'the travelling people' were moved every twenty-four hours, which meant their children could not be educated. This was gross injustice in a democracy and she knew it would have horrified Ronald. Inspired by a feeling that he was helping her she went with fists flying into what was a veritable hornets' nest.

Called the 'Devil's advocate' she discovered in a bitter, noisy, three-year-long battle that people hated gypsies because they were frightened of them. There was also a strong racial prejudice. Barbara was violently opposed at first by the Hertfordshire County Council as well as the local people who wanted the gypsies to 'jump in the sea'.

Supported by the Earl of Onslow and the second Earl of Birkenhead, she formed a Trust and finally opened her own camp near Hatfield, the first Romany Gypsy Camp in the country. The children were baptised and went to school where they all received glowing reports from the Headmasters because to them education was 'a privilege'.

But before this, almost single-handed, Barbara had got the law changed. For the first time, since gypsies arrived in England in the reign of Henry VIII, local authorities were told they had to supply camps for their own gypsies. It was a tremendous triumph although it made her a lot of enemies. Partly because of this, at the next Election, she lost the seat she had held for nine years on the County Council.

But 'Barbaraville', as the gypsies called her camp, was a victory for the justice Ronald prized so highly, and for Barbara herself it was a dream come true.

CHAPTER ELEVEN

The Queen of Health

It might have seemed that Barbara's life was full enough by now, but soon after her fiftieth birthday she discovered one of the most important roles of her life – and what was virtually a new unpaid career – as the country's Queen of Health, and patron saint of vitamins.

It was a role that she was fitted for, and one more example of the way her life now seemed to be following a pattern. For ever since the early Thirties, she had been deeply interested in problems associated with health – her own and that of others.

After the breakup of her marriage to Alexander, her nerves – despite that carefree show of outward energy – had been very much on edge, and she had suffered badly from that most agonising of internal ailments, colitis. Her doctors seemed unable to cure it, and in desperation Barbara consulted the celebrated Mrs Leyel at Culpeper, the London herbalists. This brought her some relief and started off her interest in herbal remedies, including the Chinese root, Ginseng, the legendary source of vitality and eternal youth.

Then a little later Barbara undertook a cure at Baden Baden, in the sanatorium of another pioneer of natural remedies called Dr Dengler. He was very much ahead of his time in treating his patients with unsaturated vegetable fats, which meant mainly olive oil.

Thanks to the treatment – or her constitution – the colitis went, but Barbara remained fascinated by the use of herbs and the latest discoveries in diet. This interest grew when her brother Ronald was involved in the plight of the undernourished families whose condition shocked him in the Distressed Areas and among the poor of his own constituency. Barbara began studying the whole theory of diet, in the hope of helping the children and expectant mothers in the families she visited with Ronald. It was then that she first heard about the newly-developed science of vitamins.

Owing to his frightful war-wounds, Hugh was expected by his doctors to live no more than five years when she married him in 1936. But Barbara insists that she kept him going – and in nearly perfect health – by giving him herbs and lots of honey which cured his bronchitis, and her interest in diet deepened with the war. For with wartime rationing it was not just the poor of Birmingham whose diet was impaired, but that of her own children, and one of the most important purchases she brought back from her visit to America in 1948 was a new effective, if synthetic, vitamin B which helped the whole family.

After the war, America was ahead of Britain in research into natural food and vitamins, and even in the early Fifties Britain's health food business was confined on the whole to cranks and vegetarians and bearded men in sandals. Herbal remedies were mysteriously dispensed from jars, and the public image of health food was confined to the soya bean and the nut cutlet. But according to James Lee-Richardson, the early pioneer of health-food shops and vitamins, the person who did more than anyone in Britain to promote the whole idea of healthy balanced natural eating was Barbara.

Changes were already on the way. In America, Gaylord Hauser had published his book, *Look Younger, Live Longer*, and Adele Davis had begun her important work of educating people on the role of vitamins and diet. But little of this had yet seeped through to Britain, and there had been considerable resistance to the whole idea of health-food shops.

This was where Barbara came in. In the summer of 1951 she had had a hysterectomy – from which she had taken an unusually long time to recover. Doctors had put her on to morphia, to which it turned out she was allergic, and had then tried to help her sleep with powerful doses of sodium amytal. She says that the first result of this was that she had never felt 'so truculent, so aggressive, so ready to attack anyone and everyone'. Soon she was extremely ill.

Her haemoglobin count was down to forty when it should have been one hundred and despite blood transfusions, she soon became convinced that she was dying. 'My fingers were blue and the sweat was pouring down my back.' She was so desperate that she told Hugh to get her out of hospital at all costs and bring her home to Camfield Place. She had no faith in specialists any longer. All she wanted was her own bed, a glass of good champagne, and her local doctor.

She is still convinced that this is what saved her life. The local doctor, Dr Hutchin, immediately began a course of vitamin injections and she found she had no need of specialists. Soon she was taking vitamin capsules as well, in fairly massive doses, and gradually her vitality returned. She even managed to deliver her latest book on time for Christmas publication.

As she says, she was convinced that vitamins had absolutely saved her life. 'Now,' she told everyone, 'I am going to find out a great deal more about them.'

Not long afterwards, James Lee-Richardson heard her discussing this on the radio. On the off-chance he sent her a sample of the new natural multiple vitamin capsules he was marketing, and asked her if she would help him gain publicity for a cause that could bring health and happiness to countless people – just as it had to her.

She agreed at once, but on two extremely firm conditions. The first was that it would always be left entirely to her to decide what she did or did not publicise. And the second was that she would never under any circumstances be paid or recompensed for what she did. She would promote and publicise vitamins and health foods because she believed in them and believed in doing people good. If there was any hint that she was being paid to make her recommendations, all her effectiveness would go.

For Barbara it was a test of everything she had learned about publicity, and before long it turned into her most important campaign of all. She believed her life had actually been saved by vitamins, and her belief was catching. According to Maurice Hanssen, the President of the Health Food Manufacturers Association, 'Barbara became our public figurehead, and our most effective voice. The media adored her, because she was always news, and soon she was turning what had been a rather scrappy business into a full-scale movement through her charismatic leadership.'

Lee-Richardson was equally impressed. 'I soon found that Barbara knew more about publicity than any professional publicist I'd met, and she seemed to know it all instinctively. She believed in every word she spoke, and so made vitamins and health foods a cause and something of a genuine crusade.'

Barbara's own attitude to this was simple. She had studied vitamins, and was willing to consider any product that was on the market. 'No one can bribe me. I'm too well known and anyhow, I don't need the money. I try every single thing sent to me, either on myself or on my family. If it works, I'll recommend it. If it doesn't, I won't.'

It was commendably straightforward, and increasingly Barbara began to publicise her 'cause' – on radio and television, in the press, and at public conferences. Soon she was taking on an extra secretary purely to help her cope with the individual letters for advice from the public. In 1978 she received – and answered – 10,000. She also used her influence to encourage manufacturers to produce vitamins and health-food products poorer people could afford. But here she was not always so successful.

By now she was so convinced herself of the importance of extra vitamins in the diet, that she persuaded Hugh to feed them to the animals they kept at Camfield Place – especially the pigs. She bought large tubs of Brewers' Yeast (a valuable source of Vitamin B1) from the local brewery, and fed it to the farrowing sows;

she soon found they were producing record litters. She used to mention this as a warning in the talks she gave on vitamins to women's clubs, when she was recommending Brewers' Yeast as something that could change their lives.

It is the milk of human kindness. If you nag your husband, slap your children, and hate your neighbours, you are short of Vitamin B1. The easiest way to take it is as Brewers' Yeast tablets. But one word of warning: I gave Brewers' Yeast to my sows and they all had abnormally large litters.

Many years before, Lord Beaverbrook had lectured Barbara on the need to find herself 'a platform' if she ever wanted to become a national celebrity. Her novels and her journalism had certainly got her talked about, but health and vitamins became her most important 'platform'. Once again Beaverbrook was proved right, for Barbara rapidly became a household name throughout the country.

She was indefatigable now. Indeed her energy and sheer ebullience were the best advertisement for what she preached. She had something of Ronald's power over an audience, and although she never needed to prepare a speech in advance, her talks were invariably a great success. She lectured, argued, wrote endless articles on vitamins and health, and spoke constantly on radio and television for her 'cause'. And it was now that the 'Cartland style', for which she is known to her public, emerged.

It was not really a conscious effort, though all her life she had had a horror of what she called 'beige people'. But Barbara found that her public expected her to be glamorous and were disappointed and even offended if she was not. She understood the feelings of the woman who, at the opening of a Health Store, said to her friend, 'Miss Cartland doesn't think much of us.' 'How do you know?' the other woman asked. 'She's wearing blue today instead of her best pink.'

'Barbara Cartland pink' became the symbol of glamorous

femininity, which Barbara was now convinced all women, in their heart of hearts, hankered after for themselves. The white Rolls-Royce was part of this. So were the jewels, the white fox furs, the splendid hats. Of course women followed her and she raised their standards. As the Chairman of one big meeting said, 'We have all bought new hats because you were coming.'

But there was more to Barbara's public personality than this. She had learned a lot during the war, particularly from observing her especial heroine, Edwina Mountbatten, in her public role. No woman had been more effective at winning the devotion of the civilians and the Servicemen she met at home and overseas. She was wonderful at taking trouble over the most unexpected and unlikely people. She was adept in taking a very human interest in whatever those she met were doing. She rarely forgot people's names and had a sort of genius for making them feel appreciated.

People felt better and inspired from meeting her. Barbara began to model herself now on Edwina's example, as she made more and more public appearances. She took – and still takes – great trouble over people. Thanking was important – particularly for those who would normally be overlooked. 'I expect my family to thank me for an exceptionally delicious meal,' she wrote, and wherever she went she always made a great point of thanking cooks and kitchen staff when she had eaten well.

Presents mattered too. She takes enormous pains to see that anyone who helps her, even in the most casual manner, duly receives some token of her gratitude – a gilded oak-leaf Barbara Cartland paperweight, a signed copy of one of her books, carefully inscribed and gift-wrapped with a bow of Cartland pink ribbon.

She was also developing a very positive philosophy as a public figure, which she describes as 'a sort of public Couéism', or actively encouraging the best in those she meets.

It's simply no use looking for the worst in people, for if you do you'll always find it. But if you tell people that they're wonderful, they'll probably end up by becoming it. To very rich people I want money from for a good cause I say, 'I know how generous you are,' and they *become* generous. To potentially jealous wives I say, 'Oh, but I know how understanding you are,' and they are no longer jealous. You must *suggest* to people the qualities you'd like them to possess.

When — as sometimes happened — she encountered ridicule or opposition, she would quietly ignore it or join in the laughter. For few public figures are more self-aware than Barbara. She has great personal dignity, combined with a powerful sense of humour, and can invariably turn any insult back against those who make them. As her daughter Raine says, 'It is quite impossible to send my mother up. People have tried it and it never works. She's far too clever.'

And so it was that by the late Fifties, Barbara had developed into something quite unique. When she made a personal appearance, there was a certain touch of magic to her now. She had a role, a clearcut public image and, most important of all, she was enjoying it.

As Barbara knew quite well, her increasing celebrity and fame inevitably helped the sales of her books, and it was in 1954 that she followed the success of her Regency romances with what was to prove her most attractive novel to date. *Desire of the Heart* was set in the reign of Edward VII, a period that had always fascinated her. The historical background was precise, the characters romantic and full-blooded, and the story followed the adventures of the rakish Duke of Roehampton and his arranged marriage with his *ingénue* bride Cornelia, as an escape from the scandal of a torrid love-affair with an unscrupulous vamp, Lady Bedlington.

Cornelia is a classic Cartland heroine, a Cinderella figure, who finally finds happiness and tames her wayward Duke by the power of her simple femininity. But what makes *Desire of the Heart* something of a landmark among all her books, is that it forms the

pattern for all her subsequent 'virgin and Duke' historical
romances. It remains one of her own firm favourites, and was so
successful that it persuaded her to leave the field of the
contemporary romantic novel for ever.

For she was now becoming increasingly fascinated by history.
One of her favourite writers – and one of the few authors she
actually acknowledges among her friends – is the historian,
Sir Arthur Bryant. She has unashamedly scoured his books for
ideas for her own romantic stories, but during this period she also
wrote several historical biographies herself, among them the
immensely readable *Private Life of Elizabeth of Austria*, *Metternich the
Passionate Diplomat*, and inevitably a life of the fascinating
Josephine de Beauharnais, the wife and mistress of Napoleon.

But where she was different from every other popular romantic
novelist was in the way she still combined her writing with her
public life. By now she ascribed her unabated energy to vitamins
and proper nourishment. 'Feed your brain,' she wrote. 'Cherish
your mind. Cosset it. Remember it is your most precious
possession, for your mind is YOU.'

Unlike many other devotees of health foods, she was firmly
opposed to drastic dieting. She ate well – and drank moderately –
herself, and believed everyone should do the same. For this reason
she became passionately opposed to the undermining processes of
modern foods.

My idea of Hell is to be fed meat from beef cattle which have been
given tranquillisers so that they have fattened quickly; fish which are full
of pesticides and the toxic waste from factories and sewers carried by the
rivers into the sea; chickens which have been caponised with the female
hormone, stilboestrol, so that they have been fattened like the female
eunuchs they are; eggs from hens which have been imprisoned like a
chain gang in batteries; and vegetables and fruit which have been
sprayed with poisons.

One important campaign she waged was against the compulsory fluoridation of water; and another, which she carried to Parliament, resulted in the amendment to the Food and Drugs Act to allow herbal remedies and health foods to be sold, provided their full contents were disclosed.

But through all this spate of fresh activity, the rock and centre of her life remained her married life with Hugh. Those five years of life the doctors had promised him when they married had been miraculously prolonged and she was grateful.

They were still blissfully in love, still lovers, and she ascribed this and his health at least partially to the diet she had given him – and particularly to honey. She believed in honey – as an unbeatable source of energy and as a life-giving substance

Honey is one of the most important factors in keeping people sexually competent. I promise I'm not telling you anything which is not an actual fact. I've known couples who have made love regularly into their late eighties, and I know that a great many so-called middle-aged and even elderly people, get a great deal of happiness out of love-making several times a week.

But not even honey could prolong Hugh's life indefinitely, and by the early 1960s he had been showing signs of slowing down. He was still working full-time, still enjoying life, but was beginning to think now of retiring, which was something that he dreaded.

Then, before Christmas 1963, he contracted slight bronchitis. He still insisted on going to the office every day despite appalling weather and by Christmas Day was obviously unwell. The doctor found his heartbeat was irregular. For a few days he seemed better, and was well enough to celebrate his and Barbara's twenty-seventh wedding anniversary.

Then quite suddenly, on 29 December, he collapsed and died. 'The scar tissues from the wounds inflicted all those years ago at the Battle of Passchendaele had touched his heart.'

Ronald had gone. Now Hugh had followed him. For the first
time in her life, Barbara felt she was completely alone.

She wrote a poem which she called, 'To Hugh'.

> I love the silver of the mist at dawn,
> I love the shadows underneath the trees.
> I love the softness of the velvet lawn,
> The fragrance of syringa on the breeze.
>
> I am so lonely without you here,
> You who loved everything the garden grew.
> The birds, the flowers are very dear,
> But it's an empty beauty without you.

CHAPTER TWELVE

A Star is Made

When Ronald died, Hugh had still been there to share Barbara's life, but with Hugh gone, she was on her own, and it was now that the biggest transformation of her life began.

There was nothing outwardly dramatic. Indeed, for many people, what seemed impressive about Barbara in her bereavement was the way her life apparently continued as before. There was no question of her leaving Camfield Place, nor was there any cutting back on her activities. Over the years she had had a lot of practice in hiding her emotions, and none but her closest friends could realise the gap that Hugh had left.

She had her family of course. Raine, now Viscountess Lewisham* had had two sons, William and Rupert, so Barbara was now a grandmother. Since leaving Cambridge, Ian had entered the McCorquodale family business, and Glen had gone from Oxford into the City. They were a united family.

But Barbara knew that no one could take Hugh's place. Even today, sixteen years after his death, she admits that when she is away from Camfield Place, she always gets uneasy around five o'clock, 'simply because I should be getting home to Hugh'.

Since Ian was working for McCorquodale's in Canada, it was Glen who bore the brunt of Barbara's sense of loss. 'He was absolutely wonderful,' Barbara said later. 'He stayed with me at Camfield for two years, making the tiring journey up and down to

---

* Gerald Legge inherited the courtesy title of Viscount Lewisham on the death of his uncle, the Seventh Earl of Dartmouth in 1958. He himself became Ninth Earl of Dartmouth in 1962 when his father died, and Raine became the Countess of Dartmouth. In 1976 she married Earl Spencer.

the City every day and did everything anyone could do to prevent
me feeling lonely.'

Early in 1964 Glen took Barbara on a short holiday to Italy.
They visited Naples and Pompeii, then went on to Capri, where
Barbara duly called on Gracie Fields. The last time they had met
had been in 1930 on the stage of the London Pavilion when
Barbara had shown her Albert Hall pageant of 'Britain and her
Industries' in the 'Midnight Matinée' organised by C.B. Cochran.
Barbara was impressed to see how, with age, she was more than
ever 'unmistakably and brilliantly a Star'.

Barbara returned home envying Gracie with her adoring
husband Boris and knowing that she must make her life alone. She
knew many eligible men – and had charming male friends – but in
her heart of hearts she sensed that after twenty-seven marvellous
years with Hugh, remarriage was not for her.

'If one believes in destiny,' she says, 'one cannot be defeated' –
and suddenly it was as if some pattern underneath her life were
drawing all the threads together. There were countless strands that
lay there in her past: Polly's influence and Ronald's inspiration,
her own romantic dreams, her prayers, the memory of her long-
dead love affairs. There were the lessons she had learned from Max
Beaverbrook, and the example of Edwina Mountbatten.

Above all, there was that all-important image of her ideal self
which she had put in all her books – feminine and virginal and
waiting to be loved and cosseted and borne-off to some rich
romantic world by one of nature's Dukes. It was a day-dream,
true, but it was one she knew she shared with countless other
women. And now that she was on her own, the two sides of her
nature seemed to come together. She was as much the tireless
crusader as she had ever been, but now the energy and the
ambition were directed to achieve her feminine ideals.

She worked as hard as ever, harder if that was possible, to forget
her loneliness – and in 1964, aged sixty-two, wrote six books,

including her hundredth novel which she entitled *The Fire of Love*. Interestingly it echoed a theme dear to the heart of Barbara's earliest literary heroine, Ethel M. Dell: the romantic plight of a governess in a wealthy family. But, as with all the fiction she was writing now, it was set firmly in the past, in this case at the end of the reign of Queen Victoria.

She says she would have written more, had her publishers only let her. But fearful of a glut of 'Barbara Cartlands' on the market, they were strongly urging her to keep production down. And under protest she agreed.

Instead she found other outlets for her energies that year, including a revival of the sort of pageant she had put on in the Twenties, for the World Book Fair that June. She entitled it, 'Bewitching Women Through the Ages', and had Lady Tana Alexander as Queen Elizabeth I, Rose Keppel as Lucrezia Borgia, and Jemima Bartlett impersonating her own great-grandmother, Lillie Langtry.

More important, that same month Barbara took on the Honorary Presidency of the newly formed National Association of Health to boost and publicise vitamins and promote new health-food shops throughout the country.

A quarter of a century before, when trying to describe herself, Barbara had written, 'The truth is I am "neither flesh, fowl, nor good red herring". I am neither, entirely, an intense writer with a capital "W", a socialite, nor a pure and simple home-maker.' Since then her writing had become steadily more important in her life, but there was still some truth in what she originally said about herself. For she was beginning to emerge as something quite unique.

The sales and the output of her novels were beginning to increase, but at the same time her role as a celebrity was now becoming clearer. Thanks to her energy – and, she would insist, thanks to her vitamins – age was somehow on her side. She seemed more powerful, more certain of herself, and as she toured the country, lecturing on health and opening new health-food stores, she was becoming something of an accepted national institution.

She was the Queen of Health now. She was also something more – the living glittering embodiment of what she wrote about and what she preached. She was feminine and glamorous. She was obviously extremely healthy, and quite indefatigable. She helped people but had always managed to avoid that 'beige' exterior of the traditional do-gooder. Above all, she was never boring.

This made her controversial – but it also gave her considerable authority, for she appeared now as the living proof of her beliefs. She never had been backward in proclaiming them. In her early twenties she had been 'speaking out for youth' in the pages of the *Express*. Now she was 'speaking out' for women of all ages – in her books and on the platform. The two sides of Barbara's character seemed to be in harmony at last.

As for her private life throughout this period, her main concern was still to fill the void which Hugh had left behind.

However much she missed him, she refused to mope. Thirty years earlier, after her divorce, she had taken on the world 'with fists flying'. Perhaps she was too old for that now, but she still refused to 'sit around and say, "poor little me!"'.

Instead, with great self-discipline, she organised her time so that each day was full. Camfield Place was not an easy house to run and there were continual crises to attend to there. But writing became increasingly important to her now, and it was now too that the whole routine at Camfield Place was geared to the production of her novels.

Once they had embodied all her dreams about the future. Now they had become her very private refuge and relief. She had perfected her technique: shorter paragraphs than ever; more and more reliance on direct speech in the narrative; and the action carefully toned down so that no sub-plots or diversions could impede the fortunes of her Cinderella and her Duke. Despite the dire warnings of her publishers, she insisted on steadily producing a minimum of six new books a year.

Apart from her writing life at Camfield, and her public life as a celebrity, she allowed herself little time to relax. 'There's lots of relaxation in the grave,' she used to say, and off she'd go, effortlessly changing gear between one fresh appearance and the next.

Her family meant more than ever to her now. Polly, nearing ninety, still insisted on keeping her independence – and her home at Poolbrook – but she often spent some days at Camfield, and Barbara, telephoning her every night, still found her an inspiration.

Raine and her family were also frequent visitors, although her London life had inevitably moved away from Barbara's now. In 1958 she was elected to the London County Council in one of the closest fought results in the whole election, and she was a national celebrity on her own account.

But it was Ian and Glen who were closest to Barbara. While Ian was still away in Canada she had relied on Glen for companionship and love – and they had a shared interest in that Glen was knowledgeable on antique furniture and pictures which had always interested his mother. Then in 1965, Ian's period in Canada was over, and Barbara began to take a yearly holiday with both the boys.

It was a treat for all of them, financed by the earnings from her books, and Barbara felt that she was lucky to be able to enjoy having both her sons to herself. In 1965 they visited Hong Kong and Thailand, and since Ian had a longer holiday than Glen, he and Barbara stopped off in Tehran for a few more days to see the sights.

The next year they were off to India for the Easter holidays. Barbara had already met the new Prime Minister, Indira Gandhi, through Edwina Mountbatten, and now with an introduction from Lord Mountbatten, Barbara and the boys were invited to stay with the Maharajah of Mysore.

All of them loved India, Barbara in particular, who explained that she found there 'a calmness and an acceptance of life which are quite incomprehensible to us'. Until now, calmness and philosophical acceptance had not been particularly in evidence in Barbara's scheme of things, but she was not too old to learn; and gradually her sense of loss subsided, and she discovered a new serenity within herself. She felt that time was on her side.

During the Sixties, Barbara's English publishers often hinted that her books were out of date. Not in so many words of course, but there had been suggestions that the time had come for her to get her Cinderellas into bed *before* they married, and to adapt her stories to the tastes of a new permissive era.

Barbara had resolutely declined. It was not merely that she found the whole idea distasteful – which she did – but also that she felt perceptively that there would be a powerful reaction before long to the whole ethos of the 'Swinging Sixties'.

Already as the Sixties ended, she was noticing clear signs of this in the sales of her books. Her publisher did not appear to notice, but Barbara had always made a point of studying the figures of her sales around the world and she had already seen what seemed to be an interesting phenomenon.

If her English publishers were right, the one place where her sales should be falling off was in the Western world's most sexually liberated countries, namely Scandinavia. For the Scandinavians had been in the forefront of almost everything of which Barbara disapproved: equality between the sexes, permissive sex, Women's Lib, and most notoriously, freedom for pornography. But curiously the exact opposite was happening. Instead of declining, Barbara's Scandinavian sales were booming. The world's most liberated women wanted to read about romantic love – and Barbara's Dukes and virgins. After the sexual liberation of the Sixties, the romantic backlash had begun.

Barbara is very down-to-earth about it all.

It was perfectly obvious to *me* at any rate that people would soon get bored to death with all this so-called permissiveness, and certainly women don't want to go on reading about it forever. Apart from the fact that it degrades us, most of it is absurdly exaggerated and untrue. Walt Disney always used to say that every time they made a pornographic film, he made money, and I'm convinced that every time women look at vulgar, degrading pornography, they go out and buy a Barbara Cartland.

Buy them they already did – but not yet on the scale which she believed was possible. Apart from Scandinavia there were some other interesting pointers to the future. In India, for instance, she was selling well. 'That is because Indians of both sexes understand the importance of virginity, and every bridegroom naturally insists that his bride should be a virgin – just as in my books.'

Egypt was also loyal Cartland country. (Barbara was recently delighted to learn that not only Madame Sadat is one of her Egyptian fans but also her husband the President.) So was Turkey, where there was quite a boom in pirated editions.

But Barbara was convinced that she was missing out on the big potential market for her books which she was certain must exist in Britain and America. This feeling changed to certainty at the beginning of 1973 when she went off on holiday to Tunis. Since Ian had married in 1971, only Glen was with her, and as they went through London Airport, Barbara did what every author does and glanced along the book-racks to see which of her books were selling. To her annoyance there were none on show. In Tunis it was even worse. 'In the centre of the town there is a long street in which there are straw-roofed kiosks in which there were dozens of books by Agatha Christie, Jean Plaidy, Georgette Heyer, but again no BCs!' She was 'furious', and came back from holiday refreshed and ready for the fray.

Something would have to be done. Her literary agents still urged caution, but Barbara was on the war-path now, and caution was the last emotion that she felt. She had had enough of being lectured by her publishers on the dangers of writing too many books. Her books were what she had to sell, and if her present publishers could not cope with them, others would.

With Ian supporting her she contacted the important paperback house, Pan Books, and asked if they would care to publish ten new Barbara Cartland novels in the coming year. They said they would. But this was not enough for Barbara in the mood that she was in, and she followed this with an identical offer to Pan's rivals, Corgi Books. They too accepted.

This meant that she had set herself a target of twenty brand-new novels to be finished by the middle of 1974.

So much for Britain – what about America? Here the picture seemed less promising, for she had already been published there for two years, but there had been no advertising, no promotion, and her sales were disappointing. This was depressing for an author who was now convinced that she was on the threshold of the success of a lifetime.

But her luck held. Diane Lloyd of Corgi contacted Bantam Books, the biggest paperback publishers in the world, and told them they *must* have Barbara. They were interested – but a little apprehensive. Was this the moment for the mass sale of books as unashamedly romantic as Barbara Cartland's?

The President of Bantam, Oscar Dystel, decided to rely on the advice of his salesmen throughout the country and asked them frankly how many Barbara Cartland books they thought that they could sell. Their replies surprised him – and even on re-checking seemed fantastic.

But the salesmen's message was quite clear. Readership patterns in America were changing – fast. Books about violence, crime, and sexual permissiveness were on the wane. Women were reading more books now than men and they were tired of books written for the male-chauvinist market. What they were crying out for was romance. But where were the romantic authors?

In fact there were a number of them, but none could offer

Bantam Books what Barbara could. For in effect she now possessed a literary stockpile of more than a hundred of her own romantic novels which had never yet been published in America. There were also the twenty new books she had undertaken to deliver to Pan and Corgi in the next twelve months. As she said, 'The one author in the world with one-hundred-and-fifty virgins lying about was me.' And with those one-hundred-and-fifty Barbara Cartland virgins, she knew that she could sweep the market.

And so began one of the most effective and extraordinary sales operations in the history of American publishing. To start with there was relatively little advertising and promotion, but in the first full year fifty Barbara Cartlands, previously unpublished in America, were launched upon the market. And they sold – far beyond the salesmen's estimates.

Someone had the bright idea of numbering the books, and issuing them week by week as part of a romantic series. This was even more successful, for as Barbara knew from writing them, her books were addictive, and soon there were women queuing in the bookshops for the latest Barbara Cartland.

No one seemed to mind that the books were not about America and were all firmly set in history – rather the reverse. Thanks to the romantic boom, several million women readers were suddenly as interested in Dukes and virgins as Barbara was herself.

As Barbara explained, 'My books sold because they're true romance, spiritual and physical, while the backgrounds are *unlike* real life. Most of my readers are women who are having a tough time. They don't want to read about misery, drudgery or the kitchen stove – they see that every day.'

Before long, Bantam were printing half-a-million copies of every Barbara Cartland title. Almost exactly half a century after writing her first romantic novel, Barbara had finally arrived.

The success was pleasing – if only because it seemed to prove that Barbara had been right, and this is something she enjoys.

Her books had always embodied her romantic, feminine and spiritual philosophy of life. She had never wavered, never compromised about her own ideals, and finally it seemed that they had come into their own again. This was pleasing too.

As for her private life, this wild success made little immediate difference. 'If it had happened even ten years earlier,' she says, 'it might have changed a lot of things, but now I'm really much too old to alter my own way of life.'

Besides, she had more books to write. For her it was something of a luxury simply to be free from publishers who urged her *not* to write. In 1976 she wrote not twenty, but a record twenty-four new books. And the pattern of her life continued as it always had.

She was delighted when Ian finally agreed to leave McCorquodale's and become her full-time manager. For quite apart from her love for him, she could trust him to take care of all the parts of her success that bored her – contracts, deals, promotion and finance. All that she really wanted now was to go on writing – and for life to continue as it always had.

The things that really pleased her were still tied up with her family. There was Glen, who listened to the first version of every book she wrote; Ian and Anna with their two pretty little daughters; Raine and her four children, Charlotte, Henry, Rupert and William. Barbara had grown very close to William, her eldest grandson (now Viscount Lewisham), he had stood as a Conservative in two solidly Labour Parliamentary seats and had done extremely well.

Barbara was also delighted to have her thirty years of work for the St John Ambulance Brigade acknowledged when she was made a Dame of Grace of St John of Jerusalem.

She still had her few extremely close old friends, Mary Lady Delamere (since her divorce from Captain Cunningham-Reid, Barbara's old friend had married Lord Delamere and lived for several years in Kenya) and Edwina's husband, the Earl Mountbatten. He had always been a valued ally, a tremendous help with the attention to detail of many of her novels, and as she says, he was the 'only hero we had left.' She enjoyed his brilliant intelligence and wit and says that, like the Prince of Wales, she found him 'the most interesting, knowledgeable, exciting and fascinating man in the world.'

He, in return, until 1979, when he was murdered by the IRA, attributed his outstanding vitality and health to Barbara's vitamins.

Barbara is in the *Guinness Book of Records* as taking up more space in *Who's Who* than any other woman in the world. Only Lord Mountbatten himself has a longer entry. The last time she met Lord Beaverbrook, he told her that she was one of the few women he had known who had grown more interesting with age. And one of her real achievements is that she has managed to defy time, setbacks, suffering, and appears more youthful with the passage of the years. She has succeeded – and success is as rejuvenating as the vitamins she takes.

For – thanks very largely to Ian – the romantic boom has also been a Barbara Cartland boom. She has continued her extraordinary output – twenty new books and an Album of Love Songs with the Royal Philharmonic Orchestra in 1978. This was a new departure and something a woman of seventy-seven had never done for the first time before.

The Royal Philharmonic Orchestra had come to Barbara as the acknowledged 'Queen of Romance' to ask her if she would advise them on what love songs to play in their selection from the romantic era. She thought it a great compliment but pointed out that love songs depended tremendously for their nostalgia on the lyrics and they agreed that she could have singers.

Before she started work for them she went away on a holiday with Glen which started in Guadaloupe. Motoring over the mountains she suddenly said to Glen: 'I have a wonderful idea! Why should I not sing with the Royal Philharmonic Orchestra?'

Glen replied: 'You must be raving mad, Mummy!'

Barbara, however, had the idea in her head that she might sing like Jack Smith, the 'Whispering Baritone' of the Twenties. She came back to England and asked Norman Newell, the world-famous record producer, to come down and see her. He had just made a record with Rex Harrison and Bette Davis and told Barbara: 'You have a wonderful speaking voice, I am sure we could make a record,' thinking she would do very little singing.

However, Barbara, helped by an excellent singing teacher, her Yoga breathing and a new injection in the Health Movement called RNA, produced what Jean Rook called 'a tiny dew-drenched sexy voice', which she said 'haunted' her. It was an Album of Love Songs which brought back so much nostalgia that her listeners were inclined to tears, but at least it was something new, and Barbara greatly enjoyed doing it.

In 1979 her sales steadily increased throughout the world. A recent survey showed that thirty-nine per cent of American women had *never* read a book — but eighteen per cent had read a Barbara Cartland.

She is translated into countless languages, a film of one of her novels has just been completed and more are planned; a Health and Happiness Club which is doing well in Britain has now been copied by one in America. France is bringing out two million novels a year, Germany a book a month, a Barbara Cartland magazine will soon be on the market.

'It's only the beginning of the Barbara Cartland Empire,' Ian says cheerfully.

Most of the money that she earns goes to the Government in tax, but when she is asked why she doesn't go abroad as a tax exile, Barbara indignantly replies: 'My father and my two brothers died for this country, and I don't intend to leave it at my time of life to save tuppence-ha'penny!'

But although she has resolutely tried to continue with the sort of life that she enjoys, the Cartland boom has made one difference to her life in a way that nobody had bargained for. Unlike any other living author, it has made her a Star.

She had the first real hint of this in 1976 when she travelled to America to boost her books and found herself an overnight success. The next year Mike Wallace did a special programme on her for his television show, 'Sixty Minutes', and asked her outright: 'Miss Cartland, you enjoy being a Star, don't you?'

She seemed surprised and answered: 'Oh, but I long to be a Star. Do you think I am one yet? I adore my success because I've worked fifty years to get it.'

But in March 1979, there could be no uncertainty any longer, when she flew to the United States to celebrate the publication of her hundred millionth book, and boost the sales of her latest novel – her 251st – entitled *The Prince and the Pekingese*.

Every major television chat-show in the States had begged her to appear. Her publishers had somehow found a white Rolls-Royce for her in the three major cities and Sir Norman Hartnell's workroom had been working for months on her wardrobe,

She went to Chicago, then New York, then on to Los Angeles, accompanied by Ian. But from the moment she arrived, one thing was clear: at seventy-seven Barbara was no longer just the most prolific novelist in the world. She was a reigning Star, more powerfully herself than ever in her life before as she went glittering in Cartland pink and sequins, and flashing her extraordinary green eyes beneath the television lights.

Dick Cavett hailed her as 'Britain's Queen of Romance', and she was living her romantic role as if it were a fact of life. She seemed a glamorous survivor from the wilder shores of love, listened to with slightly wary adulation as she expounded her own feminist philosophy of happiness and health.

It was as if she held a precious secret which America, and possibly the world, had nearly lost. But it was all quite simple, she explained. It was called LOVE.

Index